INSIDE RECRUITING™

THE MASTER GUIDE TO SUCCESSFUL COLLEGE ATHLETIC RECRUITING
VOLUME II

Stephen J. Brennan, Editor

Peak Performance Publishing
Omaha, Nebraska

Other Resources by Stephen J. Brennan:

The Recruiter's Library – audio and video recruiting materials
for coaches, parents, and student-athletes.

International Standard Serial Number   1089-0068

International Standard Book Number: 0-9619230-9-1

Printed in the United States of America

10   9   8   7   6   5   4   3   2   1

Published and distributed by:
Peak Performance Publishing
A Division of Peak Performance Consultants, Inc.
14728 Shirley Street
Omaha, Nebraska 68144-2144 U.S.A.
(800) 293-1676

DEDICATION

To all college athletic coaches
and administrative recruiters worldwide.

TABLE OF CONTENTS

FOREWORD

As one of the coaches who benefited by reading *Inside Recruiting™: The Master Guide to Successful College Athletic Recruiting – Volume I*, I am honored to have the opportunity to write the foreword for Volume II!

We have all heard the most important consideration for the purchase and value of real estate is "Location, location, location." Intercollegiate athletics' answer to the top three characteristics for sustained success in a sports program is "recruiting, recruiting, recruiting."

As we all try to broaden our experience in this critical area, it is great to be able to turn to the experts to learn how they have been successful. Steve Brennan has compiled a wonderful collection of coaching advice which can help all of us recruit – both inside and outside the athletic arena. *Inside Recruiting™: The Master Guide to Successful College Athletic Recruiting – Volume II* includes numerous suggestions to help you write persuasive letters, organize entertaining and convincing campus and home visits and become the consummate recruiting coordinator. You will find articles that specifically address your needs, whether that is at the Division I, II, III, NAIA or junior college level.

Life in the '90s challenges us with information overload. Steve has lasered through the experts' body of knowledge and edited a book that will help all of us become better at building the foundation of our programs through successful recruiting.

My thanks go to the coaches who shared their ideas in these two volumes. By helping us all be better at what we do, they have strengthened the profession of coaching intercollegiate athletics – and reminded us that people are the most important aspect of what we do.

— Jane Albright-Dieterle
Head Women's Basketball Coach
University of Wisconsin-Madison

INTRODUCTION

Welcome to Volume II of *Inside Recruiting™: The Master Guide to Successful College Athletic Recruiting.* The *Inside Recruiting™* Series continues to be one of the most important pieces of recruiting literature for college athletic and administrative recruiters.

This book has been compiled to again meet the need for written recruiting materials for college coaches. With the advent of **The Recruiters Institute™** seminar and **The Recruiters Library™** mail order catalog, college coaches and administrative recruiters have the opportunity to stock their libraries with an assortment of recruiting resources. Audio, video, books and technology sources are currently available.

The authors in Volume II have over 250 years of college athletic and administrative recruiting experience combined. Coaches in all divisions…from Division I through junior college…can benefit from the articles and can glean an idea or two that can be implemented immediately into their own programs. The format again makes for quick and easy reading.

Jane Albright-Dieterle, the highly successful women's basketball coach at the University of Wisconsin-Madison, delivers an insightful message to recruiters in the Foreword. She says "recruiting, recruiting, recruiting" is the most important characteristic of a successful college athletic program, just as "location, location, location" is to the real estate agent and buyer. She finishes her opening comments with a strong endorsement of *Inside Recruiting™* as an important source for college recruiters.

Inside Recruiting™: The Master Guide to Successful College Athletic Recruiting – Volume II continues to be the only book of its kind for college recruiters. As can be expected, Volume II contains a plethora of timely and unique topics to aid the college recruiter. The *Inside Recruiting™* Series has become the "bible" for college athletic and administrative recruiters looking to find the "edge" in locating and securing the '90s student-athlete.

— *Steve Brennan*

ACKNOWLEDGMENTS

I want to sincerely thank my staff of Bridget and Jon for their professional handling of this project to its completion and to Gary Anderson at the University of Nebraska at Omaha for the use of the photo on the front cover. I am especially thankful to the wonderful coaches whose articles make up this book.

Finally, I want to thank my team, Lorna, Anne, Brad and Stephanie for their continued support of Dad's projects.

Division I Championship Recruiting Methods

by Jane Albright-Dieterle

I was a high school coach for four years. During that time, I had one high school All-American. I probably learned a lot about recruiting just from what the people did to get that young lady to go there. After that, I was at Tennessee. I don't know how much I learned about recruiting there. It was more that the head coach, Pat Summitt, figured out who she wanted and then called them. She would say that's not true, but it seemed that way. Then I was at Cincinnati for a year as an assistant.

When I went to Northern Illinois University, the rules were a lot different than they are now. Some of the younger coaches are getting in at a time when the recruiting rules have changed and they're finding recruiting to be a lot harder. When I was coaching then, you could be much more creative. Now it seems like everything's illegal. A lot of things I used to find very successful, the rules won't allow me to do now.

Making the Connection

The first phase of recruiting is connecting with the recruit. When you are 40-something, connecting with a 17-year-old at the exact minute she wants to connect with you is pretty hard. Particularly, when you only have one phone call a week. So we have to have a lot of methods to figure out how to connect, because if I (as a head coach) don't connect, I'm lost.

My assistants help me make the connection. They'll tell funny stories about me, like about my tendency to kill my fish in the aquarium. They'll talk about all these different things to help me relate to the athlete. But like much of recruiting, the things you try are more concepts than an exact method. I think if recruiters understand the concepts that are used, they will better be able to attract top recruits to their programs.

Second, be yourself. To do that, you have to know who you are. If you don't have a good sense of yourself within the course of recruiting, you can't recruit. It really doesn't work. It's the same thing with your coaching philosophy. You may recruit a different style than other coaches, and that's okay. Don't compare yourself too much to other coaches. You might look at another coach who just signed the best player in your conference. You watch what he or she does and then try to do that and it just doesn't work.

My first year as a high school coach, my basketball team was 3-17. The only person I knew in town at the time had just won the state championship. So I watched her coach a couple of games and I saw her yell and scream and holler and spit. We kept losing, and by Christmas I was thinking maybe I should change my personality. So I came back from Christmas break yelling and fussing at my players. It really didn't do anything but give me a stomachache. It didn't make us any better. But I looked at that other coach and tried to do what she was doing. It didn't work. Be yourself, both in coaching and in recruiting.

Integrity is also an important thing. You have to know who you are and what you want to be. You have to be who you say you are. If you aren't, it will catch up with you. In a word, that's honesty. My father used to tell me if I always told the truth, I would never have to remember what I told anybody. That's especially true in recruiting. If you give the recruit an honest answer every single time, that's all they ever get. But if you tell them something that isn't true to get out of a conversation, then I think you're in trouble. Don't gloss over your shortcomings. There are certain things in recruiting I'm not very good at. Just like in the game of basketball, I try to work on my weaknesses and then get really, really good at the things that I *can* do.

Being honest with the recruit is very, very important. Sometimes, in conversations, I tell recruits things that are hard for me. Not really deep personal things, but about things that have happened. For example, if we lost a game, I might talk to them about it. I'll talk about how we didn't have a good February, and give them the reasons why I think we came up short. I don't just ignore the fact that we lost games at the end of February. I think that makes me a little more real to them.

> **"Building an identity for yourself is important."**

Building an identity for yourself is also important. For example, if you have a distinctive voice, it can work to your advantage. You are immediately recognized when a prospect hears your voice. It's the same with pets; when my dog hears my voice, he knows exactly who it is. Living in Madison, most people know my voice more than they know who I am because I have a kind of "hick-country-Southern" voice. It's important right away to get a recruit tuned into who you are and make a connection.

Make An Impression

I also make an impression with our stationary. On envelopes, I always just write "Jane" up in the left-hand corner on any note I write the recruits. I think that's really important. You've got to make it easy for prospects to identify your personal style. Then the prospects kind of identify with that. It can be that you're kind of funny. It could be corny jokes. I've had recruits who like jokes. If I know that, I'll always have a really stupid joke ready when I call. They'll make fun of me and laugh, but they know before I get off the phone, I'm going to tell them a stupid joke. It's just something that I do to build my identity with recruits.

Part of building an identity is setting yourself apart. Something we've been successful with in Wisconsin is using a logo consistently. We came up with the term "Badgerball." Everything we send out has this little Badgerball logo on it. I've had recruits cut the logo out and paste it or tape it on the letter when they write me back. Almost everything prospects see has a logo on it. But it doesn't have to be a logo. It could be something that you create. When I was at Northern, we didn't have the finances to do anything fancy. But you don't have to be fancy. For example, whatever your logo colors are, use that color of pen to write prospects. Most people use black or blue ink. If your colors are green, you might use green ink. Use anything that helps prospects identify with you so they will think, "Oh yeah, I recognize that." If you have ever seen pictures in the paper of the recruit's letters that they are getting that are stacked a couple feet high, you know what you are up against. How can you set yourself apart? Be the one who the prospects say, "I know that one. That's the one who always writes in green ink."

After you know yourself, really get to know your prospect. It requires gathering information and observing. When you're recruiting someone, they have different reasons for wanting to go to your school. One person may be coming to your school wanting to get their education paid for. They may be the best player in the state. They may want to go to school just to play ball. They may like to hang out with people. You need to know why this person wants to go to school. What are their goals, both short-term and long-term? Is this somebody who wants to be in the Olympics? Do they want to play pro? What are the goals that they have? You really need to understand that because you then focus everything you do to help your recruit achieve those goals.

> **Gather information about your prospect to use during the recruiting process.**

Significant Others

Relationships are another key thing. Who are the significant others in your prospect's life? If you don't know that, you won't be able to recruit them. When I was at Northern, there was a great player who was choosing among three schools, an SEC school, a Big 12 school and Northern Illinois. I knew everything about this girl, including her best friend's name.

Sometimes other schools assume a prospect wants to come to their school for a certain reason, and that turns out not to be the case. It came down to us and the SEC school. On the last day of recruiting, I was sitting at the gym with the SEC head coach. There was a girl on the bench who had a neck brace on. It was the recruit's best friend. I knew the story. This was back when you could call prospects all the time. I called every day asking, "How's your friend doing?"

The other coach asked me, "What's wrong with that girl on the bench? What's wrong with her neck?" I knew at that moment that I was going to sign that prospect. The other coach didn't even know the prospect's best friend. She didn't know that the girl had spent the last week worrying about her friend. She thought her best friend was going to die.

So know the significant people in your prospect's life. You can't guess who the significant people are. Your prospect may hate her mother. You can't try to change that. But if you know they hate their mother, don't talk to them about their mother. She's not significant. It really doesn't matter. When the prospect gets to your school, then you might tell her, "You really need to give your mother a break," but it isn't something that you can deal with before then.

> **"If the prospect wants you to meet somebody, that person is going to be helping make the decision."**

Most 18-year-olds don't have a very long list of significant others. They think everybody's significant. They'll talk to you about everybody in their school. The best way to get to know significant others is to go to their school on a school visit. Find out who they talk about. Who do they say, "You know who I want you to meet? Come meet this person." When the prospect wants you to meet somebody, you know that's a significant other. If you go meet the math teacher, the math teacher is going to be in on that decision. The kid may not know it, but the math teacher's going to help.

Spirit of Person

Next, get to know the spirit of the person; what makes the person tick. I had a player at Northern who wanted to own a Mercedes. Her goal in life was to own a Mercedes. She had a Mercedes charm, a Mercedes shirt, Mercedes everything. She wanted to play ball to get a scholarship so she could get out of school, make money and own a Mercedes. That was absurd to me. But I never told her that. I would just talk about Mercedes cars, because that was what she was interested in. You know what, once she got to school, she forgot about the Mercedes. It wasn't really a teachable moment, but I knew her spirit was about more than a car. If you don't know their spirit, you will never connect with them.

Values are important. We all have different values. As a coach, when they come to my program, it's not really my right to say, "This is good, this is bad." But kids want to talk about values. I signed a recruit from Chicago who was one of the top players in the country. I was sitting watching a game between two rival schools and my prospect decked a girl. I mean, she knocked her out. They called off the game, the cops ran in, and they rushed everybody off. The other coaches scouting her were probably thinking, "I would never touch that kid." That's what I felt. At first. But I liked the kid. I talked to her. She came to our school to visit. I said, "All right, before we get serious, we have to talk about what you value, because in this program, we don't condone fights."

She had her reasons why she did it. But most of the other coaches had written her off because she hit the other player. We all knew she could play ball. When I talked to her, she said, "I don't want to be like that. Help me. I don't want to do this." I became a person in her life that she could confide in. Values do matter. Honesty is a value. Getting a degree is a value. Fun is a value in our program. We tell them right off the bat, we have a list of 12 values in our program. We're going to have fun. We will have fun, that's a value. You might have a prospect who doesn't want to have fun. I tell them, "Maybe you should go somewhere where that's not a value."

Teach Values

Don't just preach values, *teach* values. When you're recruiting players, don't try to teach them then. Just have confidence that when they sign with you, then you become a significant other, and you can teach them. I had a recruit one time who came to a Saturday morning practice. We give our players fruit and juice before practice because most of them don't eat, even though you could tell them a hundred times to eat. This recruit was a spoiled brat. Spoiled rotten. My assistant came to me and said, "Jane, this girl doesn't want to eat her muffins. She wants bacon and eggs." I said, "Go get her bacon and eggs." My assistant said, "Yeah, right, like we'd ever do that for our players." I told her, "Leave practice. Go get her bacon and eggs. We'll teach her later that if bacon and eggs aren't on the table, you don't have bacon and eggs." But it wasn't the right time. If I'd sat down there and said, "You know what, if ketchup's not on the table, don't ask for the ketchup."

That's how I was brought up. You want the ketchup in the South, you don't ask for it if it's not there. This kid would not have understood anything I was talking about. But once she got there, we laughed and laughed about bacon and eggs. I see

her today and I say, "Have you had any bacon and eggs lately?" because she knows that wasn't a good thing. But at that particular moment, her key value was that she wanted a hot breakfast.

Focus on the Future

Get in touch with a recruit's future plans. Talk to these people about "forever." They are going to be part of your program's family. Their degree is going to be from your university. That puts them in a special mode of people. It is important to show them examples of players, in your program and your school, who have gone on to greater things. It doesn't have to be a famous person.

I'm sure at North Carolina they talk about Michael Jordan until they're blue in the face. It doesn't have to be a person like that. It may just be a player who is now a doctor. But knowing a recruit's future plans is vital in understanding where they want to go and how they will fit into your program. Make them understand this decision isn't just for the short term. This is a life-long decision. You want them in your life. I tell my players, "I don't know how long I'm going to be here – probably a while, but your degree is always going to be from this university." My degree is from Appalachian State in Boone, North Carolina. I still get alumni magazines from them. I may not know what their record was in basketball last year, but the degree will be with me forever.

Recruit the Community

> "Do something to become acquainted with the community."

You're not just recruiting this individual for your program, you are recruiting the community they are from. When you're recruiting somebody, recruit their community. If you're going to this little small town, don't eat in a town 20 minutes from there and then go to the recruit's house. Go to the town, walk into a local restaurant. Somebody will notice you and ask, "Where you from?" I tell them I'm from the University of Wisconsin. In large areas and big cities, that won't be as effective, but in those small towns, it works. Go to the post office, mail a letter, just do something to become acquainted with the community. Let them see you. They'll talk to you and then by the time you get there that night, chances are they already know you're in town.

There was a story about how Dean Smith recruited a player, how he came to the restaurant in town and ate. He said about 75 people ended up being in that restaurant for supper because everybody heard Dean Smith was in that restaurant. It was probably the only restaurant in that town. But he was there and the whole town come to see him. They wouldn't do that for me and I don't know if they'd do it for you. But you will meet somebody in that little town, so recruit the community. When you go to recruit, attend a game where the prospect is playing. When I get to a game, I sit right in the middle of the crowd. I cheer, scream and holler – all of that fun stuff – and I get to know the people's names I'm sitting around. Get to know the community. It doesn't always work, but I think it can help.

Find Out the Prospect's Core Values

Know what matters to the prospect when it comes to choosing a school. Who matters and what matters to them. What size of school are they looking for, what position does he or she want to play, and what are his or her past disappointments or failures? The size of the school can matter. They may tell you right off the bat, "I don't want to attend a school of 50,000." Perhaps they want to play for a male coach. If that is the case, you probably won't get far. You can't do anything about some wishes and desires of a player, but there are certain things that you can present in a different way. The position that they want to play also has an effect.

Within our system, we can either have a perimeter player or a post player. Tell them that is where you're going to have to put them. Know what position they want. That's a big key.

> **"Talk to the prospect about how it feels when their teammates hate their guts."**

It is also important to identify past disappointments they have had while they have been playing. Talk about them. For example, if they didn't get MVP their sophomore year and they were the best player on the team. Ask them, "How did that feel? What was it like?" It's hard to be in high school – and things like that can (and do) happen. Maybe they happened to you in the past as a coach. Even if you're the best player on the high school team, it is very hard. They get ostracized.

Talk to them about how it feels when their teammates hate their guts because they're going to get to go to this school and somebody else's parents are jealous because you are not recruiting their child. How does that feel? I think this is stuff you can't ignore. If you talk to somebody about sadness they have had playing the sport, it bonds you a little bit. You probably have some sadness in your life, too. Again, they don't have to be about the deepest feelings that you have ever had or that you would only tell someone that you are close to. But if they can relate to you just a little bit, you can make a connection.

Get to Know the People in the Prospect's Life

Another key is knowing who matters in the life of that player. These people include family, friends and significant others. I think that the family is a very important thing. I like to ask other people about their family. Their mother or father might have just died of cancer three months ago. Their mother or father might have been killed violently. A parent might be in prison. You don't always know in recruiting, and you might want to know these kinds of sensitive issues as a coach.

See if it's a close, normal family. I don't know if there is such a thing as a "normal" family, though. But don't start asking hard questions immediately, particularly with divorced families. You can't ask the typical questions, like "What's your mom do?" or "What's your dad do?" You can't do it. Because they may say, "I haven't seen my dad in 15 years." You take yourself off the list if you ask the wrong question. If you know what the situation is, you can say, "I heard your dad left you when you were in the fifth grade. That must have been pretty hard."

That way the kid knows that you know a little bit about them. They also know they're important enough that you've asked somebody else about who they are and where they come from. They don't mind. You may feel like you're spying on them, but in my experience, they seem to be receptive to that.

You must discuss with the player the chance of advancing on the team. They may want to know if they will play as a freshman. Talk to him or her about your seniors. Talk to them about their chance to advance. Everybody wants to advance. We all want to get better at what we're doing. Talk to them about that. How do they want to advance? What do they want to do? I tell them I think I can develop them at a particular position and that we can teach them what they need to do to succeed at that spot. So what if they can't jump. I can teach them how to rebound. The best rebounder I ever had couldn't jump. Everybody else had been telling her, "You can't jump." We told her what she could do.

Organizing Your Information

> **"We use a criteria form to collect information about each recruit."**

Paper drives me nuts. We have different assistants and by the time a sheet of paper is passed around, it's too late to act on it. If I have a need to know something, I usually end up looking at 800 pages. I've taken to organizing my information based on a technique used by author Harvey Mackay. He writes books on salesmanship. One of them is called *Swim with the Sharks.* In that book, he introduces something he calls his 100 questions. "Mackay's 100 questions." I have modified it to collect the information we use. It's really like a criteria form and it collects significant data about each recruit.

This is information that I think is really important and I know exactly where to get it. If I'm in a jam on a phone conversation, I don't have to look to the fifth page of whatever. This is really one of the best things we have created to organize information. The form gets to the real heart of the matter – their birth date, nickname, state, where they grew up, and shoe size. It also collects family information. Brother, sister, where their siblings went to college, and whether they went to college. Then, we collect the prospect's personal information. Interests, best friends, other friends, and favorite sports teams. If you know somebody's favorite player, you can use that information. If you know who their favorite people are, tie that in. Know what they're proud of. What religion they are. Where they work. What kind of car they drive. Guys are into their cars. I think that's significant. Mention the old Mustang. Talk about cars – maybe they think the kind of car you drive is corny. Let them laugh at it. Know their favorite meal. Hobbies. Pets.

I like to know if they like pets. Pets are almost always a connection with anybody that I'm talking to. Even when I write recruits, I send them photocopied pictures of my new puppy. I've got kids writing me back saying, "Well, I've had a snake, two parakeets and in the fourth grade..." People love to talk about their pets. Ask about them. If they don't have a pet, find something else you can talk about. But use a form to collect that information so you always have it in one place.

Another thing you can do is ask them what books they're reading. You know, I've read some of the worst books in my life because a 17-year-old is reading them. One year, I read *How Stella Got Her Groove Back*, the book about the woman who went to Jamaica. I got through the whole thing and every recruit that was reading it thought I was hip, because I knew what had gone on in it. My assistants couldn't believe I read the book. I read it because my recruits were reading it, and it gave me something to talk with them about. Some prospect will inevitably be reading the classics. That's always a little scary if you have to go out and buy *Moby Dick.* But read it anyway so that the next time you talk to them, you can talk about it.

Collecting information is the most vital part of the process. What other sports they play. Who will have the most influence in the decision about where to attend? Who has been to see them on home visits. Who else they're visiting. Where they have made their campus visits. Where they are planning campus visits. Who are we competing against? Who else is trying to get her? (I don't ask the recruit that question. I ask her coaches or her mom or dad.) The reason why I don't ask the recruit is because I don't want them going to another coach and saying, "The coach at Wisconsin was asking about you," because other coaches sometimes play this game pretty funny. They can pit you against anybody.

> **"Collecting information is the most vital part of the recruiting process."**

Work Your Plan

So after you have gathered your information, then you have to create a plan, a system that you can use to work towards the signing date. If you don't have a plan with each recruit, you're not going to be successful. What you do to get one prospect to sign might completely turn another recruit off. You can still be who you are within this system, but you have to have some strategies in place.

Take a sincere interest in him or her; don't just be interested in talent. The best players in my life that I've signed, I never talked to about basketball. We talked about everything *except* basketball. I didn't call them when they played to say, "How many points (or rebounds) did you get?" Occasionally that might come up. I was more likely to ask, "What's your life about?"

Everybody else is talking to them about camp, what they did here, what they did there. I'm talking to them about their dog, their car, movies, books – whatever. And they like me. Now, despite the fact that they like me, they still might not choose my school. But I'm on their mind nevertheless. I don't have to ask about how the game went. I have other sources to ask about her skills. I call and ask, "How'd she do last night?" If she had 35 rebounds, I might mention it. They know you care because you took the time to find out how they did.

You need to give a prospect not just your time, but also your attention. If you're just giving someone your time, it really isn't enough. If they say their favorite basketball player is John Stockton and if you remember you read a story about him two years ago in *Reader's Digest,* then go to the library, copy it and send it to the recruit. It will take some effort to do that, but do it. They know you didn't just happen to have this article on John Stockton. Anytime you go the extra mile and give extra attention, they will appreciate it.

The Written Word is Very Powerful

> **"Every letter you write is likely to be read 10 or more times by your prospect."**

What you do with your correspondence is very important. The letters that you send are going to be read by the recruit many, many times. That's just the evil of what we do. It's also going to be read by many people.

When I coached the USA basketball team one summer, I was sitting by the pool with one of the best players in the country. I took out my recruit notes and began writing. It was just another note to me. The player said to me, "You had better watch what you write on that." I asked, "What do you mean?" She said, "First of all, that kid's going to read your letter about 10 times. Then she's going to show it to everybody else."

I started thinking about that. I hadn't thought that anyone would ever read a letter I'd written 10 times. Most of them just seem pretty much like a normal letter to me. I don't know that all my recruits read their letters over and over, but I started thinking about that and started trying to be a little bit better in my letter writing. The player told me, "You've done this a million times. This is their only time." That letter is what is connecting your recruit with you. So it is very important. You don't ever know where the letter is going to end up.

There was a player in Wisconsin one year that had several of her recruiting letters published in the local paper. She didn't end up at our school. We had written her pretty nice letters, and I was very thankful that we'd written her some decent letters anyway rather than just the form letters that you might be tempted to write. Take care of the people in your state. That's where it could show up in the newspapers.

The quality of the institution where you coach is another factor. When I was at Northern Illinois, I was right in the middle of Big 10 country. I was recruiting against all of those schools. Those schools would have recruits come to football games and they would show them all of their nice facilities. At Northern Illinois, we didn't play football. I would say to recruits that "The best things in life aren't *things*." I would almost always close conversations with that expression. We didn't have a lot. We had a place to play in that really wasn't all that great. It probably wasn't much better than their high school gyms. However, at Wisconsin, we have some nice things. We have a new $80 million arena. But I still never make recruits think that is why they should come to Wisconsin. The reason they need to choose us is because of the people. People are always more important.

Make the Right First Impression

Lead off with your best shot. That's the first impression you want to make. Save your second best shot until the very end. I don't think you can play your whole hand. It's going to be a marathon with the recruit. The first letter they get from you has got to be your best shot. Your first phone call has to be your best shot at it. But be sure to save some tricks in your hat, some creative things, until the very end of it, because you're going to need something when it gets down to choosing between you and two or three other schools. If you use all your tricks in getting down to the final five, you don't have any more to use when the time comes.

At Wisconsin, the very first thing we send out is a slide show. We take a series of pictures and write them a note based on whatever the popular song of the year is. One year, it was "One Moment in Time." We told them to get out the popcorn. We included funny pictures and basketball pictures. We told them this was a slide show. We might

> **"Prospects told us, 'Oh yeah, you're the ones who sent the slide show.'"**

do something corny in it, or something serious. We almost always got a reaction. They would say, "Oh, yeah, you're the ones that sent the slide show." We didn't wait until the end of the year to send that. It was the first thing they identified us with.

Keep the Prospect's Expectations Reasonable

Don't oversell yourself. When you oversell something, it looks like an act of desperation. They can almost hear the desperation in your voice. Try to build your long-term credibility. I think that's very important, because you don't just want to be in coaching for one year. There's something to be said for consistency. Sometimes it's a factor totally out of your control.

I knew someone who chose a school because a high school coach had been to that college before several times, and he liked the people there, and he thought it was just time to send someone to that school – and that's where he recommended his star player to go. That recruit broke every freshman running record in the nation. You may not get the prospect you're recruiting, but down the line, you'll still be able to call, and if they remember that you were fair, and nice and true, that will all come back to help you. It definitely will.

In that spirit, help other players in the school besides the one you are recruiting. That's something I think is really important. Help each other. On the average high school team, how many Division I players are there? Now, how many are you looking at? One, maybe two players. That's a lot of overlooked players. So help those players out. You have friends who coach Division II and Division III. You've got friends at a different level. I have personally helped place players in schools all over the country. We've helped people walk on at a Division III school because they were a teammate of a player I was recruiting.

> **"Your job is to help people – not just to recruit a team."**

It can also help get the high school coach on your side. It takes a lot of time, but they know you're interested. If you start helping, they like that. High school coaches always want you to want everybody. This way, you're doing your part. You'll feel better too, knowing you've helped. Don't go in with the attitude, "This is the only kid in your program that's worth anything." Instead, if a coach points out another player, politely say, "We don't need a point guard this year, but I think probably she could play Division II. I know somebody who might be able to help." Then the coach thinks, "They must be all right." And, of course, you're helping that player get an education. That's a really neat thing.

But make sure when you are doing that you are sincerely interested, because if you're just doing it to sign a player, they'll know it in a second. If you don't get that player, the next year when they call and say, "You remember that player you saw when you were here to recruit that other player? Well, could you help us?" You should respond, "Absolutely, I'll help you." That's your job. Your job isn't just to get your team; it's to help people. To get them in places where they can succeed.

Relationships Are the Key

Developing good relationships with high school coaches and other people in a position to influence recruits is essential. You never know what's going to happen. One of my coaches from Northern Illinois got a job as an athletic director. He's moved all over the country, and he still calls me to ask, "Who do you think I should hire? What should I do?" You can, in the long run, help people. He knows relationships are important to us.

But make sure the coach is leveling with you. They may think they are helping you, but if they are sending you mixed messages, it can be a bad situation. On one of my first recruiting trips at Northern Illinois, I went to one of the very best junior colleges in the state. A woman there had called me and said, "I have a player for you," and I was so excited because I'd been trying to get in there for about three or four years. I went down there to watch a game and the player never got off the bench. She didn't play. I went up to the coach afterwards and said, "It's kind of interesting she didn't play tonight."

She said, "Well, she's really good, though. I think she really would help your program. She's exactly what you need." She was telling me about a player who didn't even get off the bench, who didn't get to play. What do you think I thought? I never went to that junior college again.

While you are working to develop relationships outside your office, also take time to work on internal relations. Show harmony on your staff. You have to demonstrate to your recruits that your staff gets along, that you are all one unit. Now, you may not hang out with the head coach. You might not eat with him. You might not talk to him or her when you're not at work. But you have to have harmony or your recruits will pick up on it. If you don't have harmony, it's like "something's wrong with the family." It should be a unit.

How can you show harmony on a home visit? You need to talk. Tell them what you do as a group. "Last night our staff got together for supper at…" or "Yesterday, our staff went out and…". Recruits like that. They like knowing that you like each other. They are scared if they don't know if you like each other. If you never mention the other coach, that's weird. It may not be on purpose, but it comes across as a lack of harmony. Show you get along. Support one another.

Be Creative

When you think you're running out of ideas, sometimes you can get your most creative ideas. One of the funny things we did one spring was a prom-related theme. One of my assistants got out her prom picture from a while back and photocopied it. It was her and her little date. We sat down and wrote the funniest letter you've ever seen. We made fun of everything. We got lots of letters in response. "I was the prom queen." They identified with the prom theme. We were afraid we were going to have a bunch of prima donnas in our program, thinking they had to be a prom queen. It was a creative idea, and it worked.

> **"Use themes and concepts in your recruiting to build consistency for your recruits."**

Use themes and concepts in your recruiting. We use the concept that everybody we are recruiting is going to be a person first, a student second, and an athlete third. My assistants know that. I tell them that is our order of priority. We even use it when talking to prospects. I might talk about the person part and then I'll say, "You know what, Sue's going to talk to you about the academics, the student part. That's what we told you in our home visit was the second most important thing." We reinforce the three-part concept throughout the recruiting process.

Use their name often. Everybody loves to be called by name. Use their names in their letters. Be creative anytime they have a name that you can kind of play off of.

I recruited a girl whose name was Obringer; that was her last name. When she came on her visit, we had a big cake for dessert that said "O Bring Her Here." That was a takeoff on her name. She loved it. She had us take a picture of it.

It really bothers me when people call someone "the recruit" when they could take the time to learn the person's name. That gets on my last nerve. I hate it when someone says, "The recruit left about 10 minutes ago, coach." I tell them to call the recruit by name. Use their name, don't say "the recruit." I tell them, "Go say you have to go meet Sally at the airport." Give these people names.

> **"Don't forget to have fun – or you will forget to *be* fun."**

Have fun, dazzle them and fascinate. Just don't be too serious. Recruiting is too serious. If we don't sign a prospect, we think we're going to lose our job. We look around the country and see people that have lost their jobs because they didn't get one recruit. I'm sure they are thinking, "If I'd just gotten this one player, I think I could have made it." They are wrong. It doesn't come down to one recruit. So don't go into it with an all-or-nothing attitude, or you will forget how to have fun – and how to be fun.

That doesn't require being outrageous. I'm not really a very outrageous person, but I can be fun. One year we recruited a young lady who was Player of the Year in Oklahoma. She wanted to be a doctor. We picked her up at the airport. I had on a surgeon's mask, surgeon's gloves, the whole outfit, everything like I was a doctor. Everybody in the airport didn't know what to say to me. They just tried to talk to me like I was normal, even though what I was wearing definitely wasn't normal. The recruit got off the plane and went crazy. She loved it.

But it didn't work. We didn't sign her. She went to Stanford. She did fax me all year long. Sending me notes, asking how we were doing, saying "I hope your season's going well." When we play Stanford, she'll probably score 30 points. She'll be pointing at me and saying, "That's the one who dressed up like a doctor. I'm glad I didn't go there." Actually, I don't know what she is going to say, but she knows who I am. I am the one who was the doctor. Being outrageous can work – but it doesn't always.

Get the Parents Involved

Try new things. Scavenger hunts. Cartoons. We found a couple of our recruits one year loved cartoons; they even drew cartoons. Mothers can tell you things like that about them that they don't really want you to know, like that they draw or doodle, they do cartoons, or that their favorite character is Elmer Fudd. Find out something when the prospect isn't home by talking to mom and saying, "I want to play a joke. Tell me what I can do. Help me out." Parents sometimes love that kind of thing. They can help you be outrageous if you don't really have much outrageous-ness in you.

One year at our banquet, one of my assistants got the idea to write and get the baby pictures of everybody. We had a male manager who's the nicest, sweetest, cutest, shyest guy in the world. His parents sent us a naked picture of him for this banquet. You would never think they would do something like that. But parents will help you. I don't know that they'll do that with a recruit, but get them involved.

Structure Versus Instinct

Is there such a thing as being too organized? Yes, if it makes you too rigid. You have to choose between formal structure versus instinct. I'm pretty much an instinct person. I tell people, "Sometimes you just have to throw away all this structure stuff and just have an instinct." You don't want to get so caught up in "ABCDE" – following the steps of a process you've created – that you lose your personality. All of a sudden it might hit you that you are becoming too regimented. You're sick of using the informational folder to make those phone calls. So do it without the folder. Just talk to them about whatever's going on. It is possible to get too systematic.

Even though you are recruiting different individuals, it's likely that their tastes and wants will be somewhat similar. I have a little exercise I use to demonstrate this. In your head, think of the following things:
1. I want you to think of a piece of furniture. Remember what you're thinking of.
2. Now I want you to think of a flower.
3. Next, think of a color.

Time to compare thoughts. For a piece of furniture, did you say "a chair"? Statistics say about half of the people will say "chair." Did you say a rose for the flower? It's supposed to be a little more than half of the people will think of a rose. The most frequently thought-of color, believe it or not, is red. In Wisconsin, approximately 99% of the people say red. I don't know what the connection is, but it's significant. My point is, everyone comes from different backgrounds, yet we all can think of things that are similar.

You might be thinking, "Well, players are still different." They're different in a lot of areas. But you have to find out what they're similar in and how they're different. You have to know both things. You've got to know things about them that help you understand them as people. It's always fun when I find something about a 17- or 18-year-old that is similar to me.

> **"Everyone comes from different backgrounds, yet we are all similar in some ways."**

Also, get to know the things that are different. Your players may love country music. I had a player from Iowa several years ago. On the home visit, we went to a CD store. We went in there and I got a crash course in what was popular in country music. I knew it all then. I told her, "Pick out a CD. I'm going to buy it."

When she came over to my place during the campus visit, that's the music we listened to. That is what you have to do – get to know what is similar and what is different about your recruits. You can also teach them about how something that appears to be different is really similar. I told that recruit, "This is somebody I want you to listen to. Did you know that 'Killing Me Softly' was really sung by Roberta Flack before you were even born? I don't know who these people are that try to sing it now. This is how it's supposed to be sung. Listen to this." And she did. She began to understand how things could be similar and different at the same time.

"Convincing" and "persuading" are two different things. Convince a prospect to come, and then persuade them to sign with you. Within that, it's important to build relationships. My recruiting philosophy is, "Make it so they can't say no to you." I've gotten more players because of that philosophy. They weren't going to say, "Jane, I'm not coming." Conversely, I've lost prospects who have never told me they weren't coming. They had their mom call because they couldn't tell me themselves. That's not a lot of fun. But you want it so that they just cannot bear to tell you, "I'm not coming." I'm sure I've even signed some players specifically because they couldn't bring themselves to say, "Jane, I'm not coming." I remember one player who just wasn't going to tell the world she said no. There's nothing wrong with having a philosophy like that, if you can do it.

Final Thoughts

Help the player visualize himself or herself at your school. One of the things I do with them when it gets down to the end and it's between a couple of schools is I say, "Okay. You're watching a video. Who are you playing for? Who's coaching you? Who is it?" I'm encouraged if they say, "I think it's you." I get discouraged if they see themselves in another uniform. But I don't give up. I once asked a player to visualize herself playing and she said she was playing in the Olympics. She didn't really get my point. She had skipped to another level of who she was.

If you don't sign the prospect, be a gracious loser. It can make you sleep better. It might not help you get any recruits, but you will sleep a little better. Plus, you never know who's going to come back. Things don't always work out for a player, and if you were gracious, they just might come back to you.

Author Profile: Jane Albright-Dieterle

Jane Albright-Dieterle is the head women's basketball coach at the University of Wisconsin-Madison. She has 18 years of college recruiting experience, has won Coach-of-the-Year awards in the Big 10, Mid-Continent and North Star Conferences, and has coached USA teams in the Jones Cup, World University Games and Pan American Games' international competition.

by Gary Bargen

No matter what level you're recruiting on – Division I, II, or III or even in the NAIA or junior college programs – you have to be organized and you have to develop a system.

I coached basketball at the junior college level for 17 years at two different schools before coming to the University of Nebraska to head up Coach Danny Nee's recruiting program. When I arrived in Lincoln, Danny asked me to coach, scout and establish a recruiting system. He asked me how I had handled those duties while at Hutchinson Junior College.

It was quite different, of course. At Hutchinson, I had one assistant coach who taught full-time, 15 hours a week. He traveled a little bit, mostly scouting the in-state players. Other than that, I just organized myself, since there was nobody else.

At Hutchinson, our program was pretty well known around the country. That made our job somewhat easier. We would pick out 10-20 players across the country we wanted to recruit. We only could give five scholarships to out-of-state players, so that made our decision-making process even simpler.

At Nebraska, it was much different. It took time to create the kind of program we wanted to establish and to coordinate and organize our recruiting efforts.

NCAA Rules and Regulations

The National Collegiate Athletic Association has changed many of its rules and regulations for recruiting in the last 20 years. One of the most important things you can do in the area of rules and regulations is ~~discuss them with your coaching staff and your support staff~~.

You don't have to go into great detail with administrative support secretaries and people who answer the telephones, but they should have some basic understanding of the guidelines which must be followed. This includes guidelines for campus visits and what constitutes an "institutional representative." *Section 6.4*

Your support people should know what needs to be done to prepare for a campus visit and the ways expense accounts for the visits can be handled. As for defining institutional representatives, this can be a complicated area and it's also one where many violations occur.

Mailings/Correspondence

At Nebraska, we received plenty of letters from fans and alumni around the country informing us of players we should recruit. Sometimes these "tips" were about high school sophomores or juniors or even, in some cases, about an eighth grader. When we received a letter like this, our secretaries would oftentimes send a questionnaire to one of these prospects. However, we made it clear that they can't be sending anything other than a questionnaire to recruits of a certain age.

Correspondence with a prospect is a very important part of the recruitment process. When can you send a questionnaire to a prospect? How old do they have to be? What constitutes a questionnaire? Should you send a generic letter? What constitutes "generic"?

I know first-hand what prospects see in the mail from schools these days. After my son completed his sophomore year, he was already receiving some questionnaires in the mail. He said some of the letters made a bigger impression on him than others. I just had to find out what was so dynamite about the ones that caught his eye.

> **"All of our letters are personally signed, usually by the head coach."**

For him, the schools that mentioned they were going to be seeing him play in the near future made the biggest impression. The rest of their letter wasn't much different from what we were sending out at Nebraska. It included how the season was progressing and what was still to come.

Sometimes, you'll send out a questionnaire and it won't be returned. Don't necessarily take this to mean that the prospect isn't interested in coming to your school. Find other ways to make contact with them and gather more information.

We used two types of mailing lists: a junior mailing list and a "hot" list. All juniors on our mailing list received a letter once every 10 days to two weeks. These letters contained information related to the time of year when they went out. Oftentimes, they mentioned tests like the ACT or SAT, as well as different things about our program.

Our hot list included people who were seniors and players who were at the top of our prospect list. Oftentimes, we saw them play several times or they were junior college players we were recruiting. These people received letters once a week. We made them as personal as we could. All of them were personally signed – not stamped or mimeographed – usually by the head coach. Of course, someone else may actually be signing these letters with the coach's signature since it can become very time consuming.

We also had a postcard that we sent out to recruits, asking them to fill out information on where they'd be playing. This helped when it came time to organize your summer travel schedule.

Despite spending so much time mailing out letters, there are many prospects who will never read them – especially the ones who are very, very good and receive five to 10 letters a day. When you face this situation, unless you're building a pretty good rapport with them over the telephone, you should be handwriting letters to them. But just because it's handwritten doesn't necessarily mean a recruit is going to read it. However, if there is something in that letter that you've talked about or something that's coming up and they happen to read it, it may make a difference.

Another mailing we made prior to the signing date was called "20 reasons." It's a collection of 20 reasons why the recruit should come to Nebraska. Each reason is a letter in itself. We back-dated them to the signing date. That way, they received all 20 letters by the weekend prior to the signing date. If you forgot to send one or two out, it's okay to send more than one letter out in one day; just use separate envelopes. What you put in these 20 letters is up for you to decide, but at Nebraska we tried to cover all areas of athletics and academics. This system has worked very well for us.

Telephone Calls

Generally, you're allowed one call per week to a recruit. However, sometimes potential recruits call in to the basketball office (they sometimes even call collect). The NCAA has strict guidelines on what age people can make collect calls into your office to speak with a coach. That's why it's important that the people who answer the phones know the rules.

You're allowed to make only one call to a recruit a week. Players on our "hot list" always received one call a week. Some of the others received a call every two weeks. We always tried to follow up every telephone call with a personal letter. That didn't take into account how many mailings that person had received, either. You should include something about your telephone conversation in the letter. Obviously, if you're making three or four calls a day, it isn't too time-consuming to scratch out a few letters. However, if you're calling 10 to 15 prospects a day, you won't have time to handwrite them all. I used a Dictaphone and then turned it over to my secretary to transcribe. If I was on the road, my secretary had a telephone Dictaphone system that I could dial into. That way, I could call at any hour of the night and leave the messages for her to type when she got into the office.

Identification of Prospects

One of the first processes in recruiting is the identification of a prospect. But before you start jotting down names, you should determine what your needs are as a coaching staff. After identifying your needs, you must prioritize them. What's your number one need? What team or coach doesn't need big people? But maybe you also need a point guard. To make a decision, you must prioritize what your

> **"Before identifying prospects, determine your needs as a coaching staff."**

number one need is for the first year, the second year and so on. At Nebraska, we didn't only look ahead to next year, we looked two, three or even sometimes four years down the road. We utilized a continual depth chart, which showed three years at a time.

For example, a 1998-99 depth chart shows the current 1998-99 situation – how many seniors, juniors, sophomores and freshmen we have. It then breaks them down by position. That way, you can easily see what your recruiting needs are for each position, each year. If you extend the depth chart to the following school year (1999-2000), you'll see who's graduating, who's moving up the depth chart and what your needs will be at each position. It's important for you to not only see where you are now, but what your short and long-term recruiting needs will be in the future.

Identifying Prospects

> **"It's easy to spend a lot of money on scouting services, so use those services wisely."**

How do you identify a prospect? Scouting services are probably the most common way. Nebraska subscribes to between 20 and 25 scouting services. It's easy to spend a lot of money in this area, so you should try and identify which scouting services are helping the most. Sometimes it can become almost a political process when it comes to subscribing to a scouting service. The coordinator of the service might be a friend of the head coach or he might be an alumni of the school. Sometimes your decision on a scouting service is based on what part of the country the service is located in.

Another common way to see what's available is to attend summer camps and tournaments. This is particularly important in Division I, when the NCAA allows you to scout during the month of July.

Identifying a prospect is one thing; evaluating whether they fit into your system is another. Not every superstar fits into the chemistry of an established team or program. You also have to consider how many scholarships you have available.

Organizational System

One of the things we developed at Nebraska was a card system to evaluate prospects. It used 5 x 7 cards which identified the strengths and weaknesses of each prospect: ball handling, passing, shooting, playing defense, running the court, quickness, athletic ability, etc. We also listed other things like coachability, cooperation with others, etc.

After you've been in the business for a long time, some of these evaluation points won't mean as much as others. But if you're not really sure you can get the next Michael Jordan to play for you, you're still organized enough to compete for a solid performer.

An evaluation system of this type does take a lot of time. To adequately evaluate a prospect on-site usually means doing so on scratch paper and then transferring the information onto the cards. Sometimes, we spent another hour just writing up a card on a player.

When you watch a prospect, you should have an objective method for rating them. A good test of this is if you see a player more than once. Don't rely on what you've seen the first time – start a new card. Then compare the two. Sometimes the evaluation will be the same, but sometimes it can be very different. Evaluating a player both in and out of the season is a good way to get a fair assessment of their conditioning levels, attitude and other intangibles you might not otherwise notice.

We also used a more extensive form which had a place to list all the times you saw the recruit play and practice. We also listed who had called the recruit, what correspondence we sent them and what other schools they were considering. We also had a place for directions to their home and school. This information got transferred to a profile sheet, which is discussed later on.

Signing Periods

Ideally, you'd like to sign as many prospects in the fall as you can. That way, you can spend the rest of your recruiting time during the season evaluating younger people (sophomores or juniors). Unfortunately, it doesn't always work out that way and you end up spending a lot of time during the evaluation period (December, January and February) trying to recruit players for next year.

Personal Contact

There are three types of personal contacts with recruits: in-school visits, in-home

visits and on-campus visits. There are official and unofficial visits as well.

Whether it's an in-home or in-school visit, you must have an organized presentation in place. Obviously, there's going to be times when you have to do things off the top of your head. But if you've done enough organized presentations over a period of time, then what you say off the top of your head is going to be pretty well organized as well.

What should you put in an organized presentation? First of all, it has to be an attention-grabber; something that's different from what other schools might be doing.

We started every in-home or in-school visit with a discussion period. We used a profile sheet to help with this part of the process. It contained everything we knew about the prospect: how tall he was, who his family was, his coach, the things he was interested in, telephone numbers, etc. We also included things like where he'd already taken visits or where he was going to take visits. Finally, we included the points of emphasis we wanted to make with the prospect.

We actually gave a copy of this profile sheet to the recruit, his family or his coach – whoever was at the meeting. We told them we prepared it to show them that we had done our homework. We asked them to tell us if we made any mistakes on it. The information on this profile sheet was usually extensive, prepared over the course of numerous telephone conversations with coaches, the player, the parents and so forth, over a long period of time. You'd be surprised at what effect it had on them.

> **"We give a copy of the profile sheet to the recruit, his family and his coach."**

If you made a mistake on the profile sheet, you were going to find out about it, which was to your advantage. How you handled it depended on what the mistake was.

For example, during one visit, I said something about the prospect's girlfriend and his mother about came unglued. She said, "I want you to know I don't want him to have anything to do with her. I dislike her."

I said, "Oh, excuse me. He didn't feel that way. He'd been telling us all the time that she was a pretty important part of his life."

Another important part of the visit process was a recruiting tape. The NCAA has really changed the way you can do these. But in the three minutes you have, you really have to produce something that's best for your school that is within your budget. Another factor to consider is how often to change your recruiting tape.

No matter what the cost, it's important to have a tape since some recruits may never make it to your campus.

Finally, you should have a recruiting brochure/press guide for them. At one time, the two were separate books, but that's no longer allowed. This booklet should be something they can hang onto, to read about your program.

We concluded our visits with a summary of where we thought they would fit into the program. Most of the time, this meant offering them a scholarship. Normally we wouldn't be in the home if we were not offering one, but there were exceptions to this, of course.

When you make an in-home or in-school visit, you typically only get one shot. By staying organized, you can accomplish everything you set out to do, as well as leave time for questions from the recruit, his parents or coach.

The Campus Visit

Every campus visit a prospect takes to Nebraska is supposed to be special for him. He is treated as a special guest. Like an in-home or in-school visit, you're likely to get just one chance.

The campus visit encompasses many things: academics, facilities, player contact, activities and even eating at the training table.

> **"If possible, invite the parents to the campus visit."**

We liked to schedule visits when there was something going on on campus. In the fall, football weekends were really big for us because there were a lot of people and there was plenty of things happening.

I think you have to have the best accommodations that your budget will allow, as well as what conforms to NCAA regulations. You want something that's nice, but not extravagant.

As for eating, a lot of times, that's all they do while you have them around. You should find out what kind of food they like before they ever set foot on campus.

Every campus visit should have some type of special presentation that's customized solely for that player. One of the most common is preparing a game jersey complete with the player's name and number. Although he can't take it home, you can hang it in a locker and show him where his locker would be if he decides to sign with your school.

If at all possible, invite the parents to campus with their son. You can't pay their travel expenses unless they drive, but this is a great way for them to see where their son or daughter is going to go to school. It's not always possible for them to come, but you should at least extend the invitation.

Summary

Everyone has their own system. It's important to individualize your recruiting techniques.

At Nebraska, we sat down as individuals and then as a group to decide who our key recruits would be and how we would recruit them. This plan may be adjusted along the way, but it's essential to have one in place for every prospect. Identify the most important people in their lives. Who's going to help them make the decision? Is it going to be the coach, it is going to be their mother or father? Is it going to be somebody out on the street, a third party?

We also tried to identify every prospect's "hot button." What was important to them? Was it academics? Was it graduating? Once you knew what their goals were, you could sell your program around them. Of course, if the recruit's goal was to become an engineer and your school didn't have an engineering program, you would have to figure out a way to still sell him on coming to your school.

You must also be persistent. Don't take "no" for an answer. Build rapport with the athlete, his parents and the people around him. Don't let one failure cause you to get down in the process. How many of you have ever signed every player you ever recruited? That's why you always have a long list of prospects. Maybe you're not working your 10th and 11th prospects as hard as you are the first five, but you still have to work them. Someday you might need that 10th or 11th guy. It happens.

> **"Remember to market your strengths."**

Remember, you're not going to sign everyone you recruit. Realize that and it will keep everything in perspective.

Remember, too, that your job has no boundaries. If you're at a wedding or family function and someone mentions they know a "spectacular player you should get your hands on," make a mental note of it. You may not be able to make contact with the recruit right away, but you can at least put them in your files and go after them when the rules allow. If you forget about the guy until his junior year, he might be so good by that time that you don't have a chance.

Remember to market your strengths. Find ways to make your program's least impressive characteristic be less important or seem adequate. Every school has something that's not quite as impressive.

Also, make sure your head coach is involved in the recruiting process. I tried very hard to make calls to our top people during a time of the day when Coach Nee could be there. That one call may be long, but it's only once a week.

In conclusion, sell your program. Be positive with your program rather than degrading another school's program. Stay organized. Work hard. I believe there is no other way to do it.

Author Profile: Gary Bargen

Gary Bargen has 25 years of college recruiting experience on the Division I and junior college levels. A Coach-of-the-Year award winner, his coaching stops include Hutchinson (KS) Community College, Southeast (NE) Community College, and the University of Nebraska-Lincoln. He is currently serving as assistant compliance coordinator at the University of Nebraska-Lincoln.

SELLING THE STUDENT-ATHLETE DURING THE HOME VISIT

by Theresa Becker

Recruiting is an ever-changing game. In the 16 years I've been involved with the game of college basketball, it's been amazing to see how much changing and adapting we've had to do as coaches and as recruiters – all to meet the needs of the student-athletes, parents, coaches and the public. It's definitely a challenge and it's one I think is going to continue to change and evolve.

I began my college coaching career at Furman University before moving on to Bradley University. I spent three years at Bradley under Angela Beck, who helped transition the school from Division III to Division I. That was quite a challenge because we inherited a schedule which had half of the Big 10 Conference teams while we still had Division III athletes. I found out really quickly – as a recruiting coordinator and as an assistant coach – what it means to get in the trenches and how to really work hard.

I understood this even better when I left the University of Nebraska to take a job at Iowa State. I had been at Nebraska for six years and knew the institution like the back of my hand. I was confident and very comfortable. There were very few curve balls that could be thrown at me that I couldn't hit.

But that all changed at Iowa State. We went 2-25 my first year. It was definitely a challenge, but one I wouldn't pass up if given the choice again. That's what competition is all about. We're all after challenges and that's part of recruiting.

Working With Assistant Coaches

My years as an assistant coach and recruiting coordinator for Angela Beck at Bradley University and the University of Nebraska were the best years of my life. I had a tremendous experience with her and I think the reason was because we were so different. The one thing Angela allowed me to do was develop. If you're a head coach, you should strongly consider allowing your assistant coaches time to learn and develop.

Your assistant coach is really an extension of you. You should develop him or her in that sense, with the mentality that you are ultimately the product that your assistant coach should be selling. You need to take time to convince your assistant coaches to believe in you, to adopt you and to adopt your philosophy. Then they go out and put your actions into action. That's when they truly become a recruiter. Once you identify that your head coach is the one thing you should be selling and you sell the recruit on that person, then you're on your way.

Working With The Head Coach

The first rule as an assistant coach or recruiting coordinator is to make your head coach look good. If you can't make them look good, then you can't make your institution or your team look good. It begins with the head coach.

Ultimately, the head coach determines playing time, starting time, the rules and they have the final say on everything – suspensions, releases, non-renewals.

> **"Developing a relationship with your head coach takes time."**

Developing a relationship with your head coach takes time. It's easy for young coaches to get frustrated and to be too quick to judge. It takes time to develop the kind of relationship where there's a trust and a bonding and one where there's an understanding of your limitations. That was the nice thing about Angela. She never treated me like an assistant coach because I never acted like one. I took responsibility. The more she gave me, the more I wanted.

Know Your Product

Like a good salesperson, you have to know your product. What are you selling? Your institution. Your program. Your players. Your academics. But it takes time to learn everything you need to know. The first thing I did when I got to Iowa State was to talk to people in the admissions office. We tried to absorb as much information as we could from the university catalog, admission guides, etc. Even though I came on board in May, I knew it would take a long time to be prepared for home visits in September and October.

Knowing your material well helps you relax. It allows you to sit back and enjoy yourself during a home visit with a recruit, and truly share information instead of becoming so much like a salesperson. You can talk naturally and discuss things in a manner that people can relate to, understand, and feel comfortable communicating back with you.

Selling Yourself

When talking to a recruit, you have to be up front and you have to be honest. You must be careful not to be misleading, either. If you mislead an athlete in the recruiting process, you've dug yourself a big hole. When you're sitting in a home, looking a recruit in the eye and talking to their parents face-to-face, your word is gold. You're likely to discuss important things like a starting job, or point production, or even a scholarship. Your word will be the thing that people will hold you to more than anything else.

There's obviously a big difference between talking to someone over the telephone and talking to them face-to-face. You have to be careful not to make promises over the phone that you wouldn't make while sitting across the sofa from them. If you mislead them or are not completely honest and that recruit eventually ends up committing to your school, you're going to have a bad situation on your hands later on.

If you do your homework from the beginning and really think about how you're going to present your program during the home visit, you'll avoid problems later on. Remember, be up front, be honest and try not to be misleading.

It's not only important to know what you're going to say but also how you say it. Change your voice inflection, mix up the tempo of your presentation – don't be monotonous. Most assistant coaches are former athletes who are more comfortable playing in front of people than speaking to them. If this is one of your weaknesses, concentrate on making yourself better.

> **"Recognize your weaknesses so that you can make yourself better."**

Interacting With A Recruit

How do you get the student-athlete involved during a home visit? How do you get them to talk? These are questions every coach, assistant coach or recruiter asks themselves at one time or another.

My secret to overcoming this problem is to write down every question or concern that comes to me. I make a list and use these questions to lead into each aspect of my home visit. It's a trick that's very effective in keeping me from boring my audience to death.

Another good idea is to avoid using too many statistics. I find when you become statistical, you really lose people fast. Especially if you're dealing with a wide variety of recruits from different backgrounds. Some kids are interested in statistics, others aren't. Some parents follow you and some don't. Some care and some don't. Statistics are a good way to validate information, but if you become too statistical, you can get to a point where you're talking over everybody's head.

It's also important to get all parties present involved. When I worked with Angela Beck at Nebraska, we made every home visit together. It was a philosophy that if we were truly going to sell a student and a family to our program, we felt like teamwork was the way to go.

I continued to do this at Iowa State. When you're recruiting from a large pool, it's sometimes difficult to identify the recruits who are serious about coming to your school. That's why I was adamant that we make our visits together because our recruit list was so large and we were both calling a lot of recruits and trying to establish relationships.

Assistant coaches should pride themselves in knowing their recruits inside and out. This pays big dividends when it comes time to make a home visit. It helps the recruit feel comfortable and helps you feel comfortable. Plus, when you're working as a team with your head coach, the recruit oftentimes feels relieved that you're on hand because he or she might be facing a head coach they've hardly spoken to before.

It's also important to be yourself during a home visit. Today's recruits are very judgmental and very quick. As soon as one school knows it's recruiting against another, people really start talking. Sometimes this means you'll walk into a home and the recruit already has a predetermined opinion about you and your school based on what they've heard from someone else.

Telephone Recruiting

When you can only speak to a recruit once a week, it's tough to develop any kind of relationship. It almost becomes a game as to how long you can stay on the phone with a recruit. And when you have so many kids to talk to it no longer becomes a one-man operation. That became very frustrating for me because I had always taken on all the phone responsibilities.

I wanted to know everything I could about a recruit. But when I got to Iowa State, we were recruiting so many kids, I couldn't keep up with all of them. That's why it's important to work closely with your assistants or your recruiting coordinator to keep yourself up to speed on every recruit.

Selling Your Product

> **"Look for student-athletes who are leaders – people who will be able to set the tempo for your team."**

When you're touting your program, remember to identify your weaknesses and convert them to strengths. I'll use our 2-25 record at Iowa State as an example. I sold my program as a great opportunity for a young athlete who wanted to be a part of something new.

I looked for leaders who would set the tempo, someone who wanted to be a part of a championship team. I sought out athletes who had the courage to be fierce competitors night in and night out. And I told them the going was not going to be easy. I didn't guarantee success or even a winning record. What I did promise was that I would work hard – and they would, too.

I didn't have to tell them that Iowa State's basketball program was down – everybody else in the country already was. That's why it was so important to talk about the weaknesses and what areas I wanted to improve in. I wanted to beat my competition to the punch and turn a negative into a positive.

Don't forget your humor, either. You should have fun during your home visits. Sometimes when you get so starched-collared, it's hard to relate to the recruit. A good example of this for me came during a recruiting visit Angela and I made in Pennsylvania. At the airport, Angela's bags containing her shoes got lost. She wears a size seven and I wear a 10. Unfortunately, we didn't have time to go out and buy her another pair so I had her put on my extra pair of size 10s. We stuffed the toes with tissue for a less-than-comfortable fit.

Unfortunately, our visit to the recruit's house was going equally as poorly. The recruit wasn't opening up and we weren't getting anywhere. Suddenly, I noticed the recruit was staring down at Angela's shoes. You could see her toes at the top of her shoe – that's how much tissue we had stuffed into them. Noticing that the recruit and her mom were staring at her feet, Angela broke down and told them the whole story. That's all it took for them to open them up and it became one of the most productive visits we ever had (we also ended up signing her as well).

Don't be afraid to let your guard down now and then. It's a simple thing and it shows you're human.

Planning The Visit

You learn from your mistakes. I think experience and mistakes have been my greatest teachers. That's why planning is so important.

A good recruiting visit begins with a confirmation letter to whomever you'll be visiting. This is also a good time to get directions to where you'll be going. I developed a form to write down all the pertinent information about the recruit. It's much more organized than jotting things down on hotel notepads or tearing pages out of the phone book. In addition to having the directions to where I'm going, my form also serves as a checklist and as a pre- and post-visit evaluation form.

Once you have the directions to where you're going, scout out the location in advance. This comes in handy when you have a panicky head coach or when you're

running behind schedule. I always dropped Angela off at the hotel and then ran by the school or the house to find out exactly where we were going. This is another thing that you can really do for your head coach to relieve the stress and anxiety of the presentation.

Another simple thing to keep you organized and in a good mental frame of mind is to coordinate your restroom and meal stops. It can be really tough with flight and driving schedules what they are, but you're not doing yourself justice if you're going to a visit on an empty stomach. Eat before you go into the home because being hungry can affect your presentation and your ability to focus.

As I said before, traveling in pairs has its advantages. Take a good look at each other before you head up to the front porch. Is your tie straight? Are your earrings crooked? Did you forget to put on your lipstick? How you look is just as important as what you say.

Wearing Your Pride

The way you dress also says a lot about what you believe. I'm big into wearing my school's colors. When I started at Furman University, I had to get used to wearing the school colors: purple, gold and white. In high school, I couldn't stand the color purple. So in my first college coaching job, I researched purple because I wanted to be able to feel good about it. I wanted to wear it. I wanted to believe it. It's all part of knowing your material, believing your material. This was also one of the first things I did when I got to Iowa State.

I know it's hard for guys to walk around in red suits or green shirts, but there are other ways to show off school pride: ties, school rings or even lapel pins.

Wearing your school colors says a lot. It indirectly tells the families and your players that you are really into this. It also sends a good message about what you're all about.

Packing For The Home Visit

In addition to packing all the right clothes (how about carrying an extra pair of shoes?), my staff put together folders of information for all our home visits. They included all the information we'll either talk about in the home visit or information the student or the parents have expressed concerns about. We always tried to take things along which can be referenced during our conversation with the recruit. These folders should be very thorough and contain: a game schedule, the university catalog, athletic media guide, financial aid information, graduation rates, housing information, information about the city, campus life activities, an activity calendar or even safety, security and insurance information. And most important, don't forget to include your business card so the recruit can contact you if they have any questions.

> **"Take along game schedules, catalogs and media guides when you go to visit a recruit."**

In addition to the information folders, we also put together a campus visit calendar which listed everything that was going on each day on campus and provided the recruit and their parents an idea of what were – and were not – good days to visit.

You'll find that most high school students use calendars of their own to stay organized and plan their schedules. Another thing to carry with you is a recruiting film. It's a highlight tape of your program. We always took two, just in case something went wrong with the first one. And when you call to get directions to a school or home, that's also a good time to ask whether they have somewhere to play your tape. Every once in a while, you won't have access to a VCR. So if you know this in advance, you can make arrangements to work around this situation.

Sometimes we brought along a copy of our off-season workout booklet. A lot of recruits are interested in finding out what colleges are doing and getting ideas on working out. Another good conversation piece is a small dry-erase board. If the recruit is interested in knowing where he or she is going to fit into your system, or how you're going to be utilized, this is an easy way to show them.

Occasionally, we provided an outline of our presentation to the recruit and their parents. It was helpful for them to follow along and not only hear, but see, where we're going with our presentation. You don't want to get to the point that you're extending that hour-and-a-half or two-hour visit into a four- or five-hour marathon session. Today's student-athletes have many demands and commitments, so it's important to be organized, efficient and effective in the time you spend with them.

> **"Be organized, efficient and effective in the time you spend with recruits."**

The outline also helps after you've made that 10th, 11th or 12th straight home visit and you're not sure what ground you've already covered. Don't be afraid to set the outline right in front of you on the coffee table or sofa. In some ways, it shows you're organized and most people appreciate that.

For our own reference, we also brought along the file we had put together on the recruit. As an assistant coach, if you're the one who's really been involved with the recruit's initial recruiting process, it's great to go back and look at all the phone conversations you've had. You can bring something up either as an icebreaker or just to press a point. Plus, it's impressive to make mention of something personal about the recruit that will impress them into believing you truly care about them as a person, as well as a recruit.

Another piece of paper that's integral to every visit is the evaluation form. I've developed three different types: The student-athlete form, the home visit form and a post-visit form.

The student-athlete form is for a school visit. We use it whenever we talk to a coach, a counselor or a teacher. It's divided into two areas: athletic and academic. When you're recruiting a lot of kids, the thoughts and feedback you write on this form helps you better sort out one recruit from another when it comes time to narrow your focus.

The home visit form also contains room for academic and athletic information, as well as details on travel arrangements, timetable concerns or even parent's names. It's your "cheat sheet" that can make a big difference in personalizing your visit that much more.

> **"Don't lug the NCAA manual into the house, but have it nearby."**

The post-visit form serves as an evaluation of the student-athlete and the visit as a whole. It records the recruit's response, personality and desire to come to your school. It's also a good way to record how you rated the visit so you can track how you're doing as an effective recruiter.

Finally, in addition to everything else, take a copy of the NCAA rules and guidelines manual with you. You don't have to lug it into every living room (keep it in the car), but having it nearby can come in handy when you don't know the answer to a question.

Summary

Taking time to organize yourself and your staff pays big dividends in the recruiting process. Some things you take for granted are often the things you're first to forget – and often what most people in the home visit are most interested in hearing about.

One of the greatest compliments I think people can give you is that you covered everything. When you ask them if they have any questions and they reply, "no," that's the best time to refer to your written outline form to bring up the questions that you know are concerns.

Planning, organization and good documentation are all integral keys to success in the home recruiting process.

Author Profile: Theresa Becker

Theresa Becker has 16 years of college recruiting experience. The former head women's basketball coach at Iowa State University also has coaching stops at the University of Nebraska-Lincoln, Bradley University and Furman University. She is currently serving as an assistant compliance officer at the University of Nebraska-Lincoln.

HOW TO MAKE YOURSELF INTO A TOP RECRUITER

by Tim Carter

How to make yourself into a top recruiter? First of all, I just think that you really, really have to enjoy what you're doing and enjoy being around people.

I want to share with you my experiences recruiting both at the University of Nebraska at Omaha and Northwestern University. When I took the job at UNO, I was happy to be back with the kind of players that I was used to being around. I call them, "My kind of guys." In contrast, Northwestern is obviously one of the top academic schools in the nation. At Northwestern when you got on the plane after a game, players pulled out their books and began studying. Honestly, the UNO players were more like me.

I remember my first day on the job at UNO. I was in my office when I heard one of the players talking as he was walking down the hallway. I heard him say, "I'm close." I didn't think anything about it. He walked into the coaches office next to mine. I heard another player walk out of that office a short time later. He said, "John, you're close, man." I didn't think anything about that either. About 30 minutes later I heard someone scream, "I got it!"

Getting up, I said, "Good gracious, what's going on down there?" I walked out of my office and went into this coach's office. The players had puzzles laid out on top of one of the coach's desk. I said, "What's the big deal?" The player said, "Coach, it only took us a week to put this puzzle together." I looked at the box, which was marked for ages 10-16 years. I thought to myself, "These are my kind of guys!"

When I came to UNO, I realized I had a really tough job ahead of me. I was walking into a situation where about four or five guys were supposed to have been ineligible, and two of them were talking about transferring.

Second, if you are going to make yourself into a top recruiter, I really believe that you have to know yourself. When I was at Oklahoma State, the program was at the very bottom. My boss, Coach (Leonard) Hamilton, said to me, "Tim, the reason why I hired you is because I really think you like what you're doing."

No Secrets

I don't think there are any *secrets* to being a good recruiter, but I do think you must enjoy what you're doing. If it's too hard for you to sit down and visit with a prospect or his parents about your school, or if it is too hard for you to be in large gatherings of people, I think you may be in the wrong profession. Because if you can't sit down with a mom, a dad, a sister, a brother, a basketball junkie, or an AAU coach and really enjoy talking to them, then I think you're fooling yourself if you think you're going to get into this profession and be successful.

I don't think there are any secrets to being good at what you do. I think you flat out have to enjoy being around people. If you don't enjoy that, then I think you're setting yourself up for failure. For example, I happened to be at an AAU tournament in Wichita when I saw a guy coaching his team. I just loved the way he handled the players. I went up to the him to talk about a player, but I was more interested in talking to him about taking a job with me, because he really seemed to enjoy what he was doing. His players enjoyed playing for him.

As a result of that, they were doing all the things that we all want our players to do. If you ask yourself, "Is recruiting something I like to do?" and the answer is anything but "Yes," then you might want to think about doing something else, because if your heart isn't in it, you probably won't be very successful at it.

Honesty is the Best Policy

> **"There are some who are perceived to be great recruiters, but a lot of people don't like them."**

I think, along with being honest with yourself, you have to be honest with other people. I don't think there's any substitute for telling kids and parents the absolute truth. If you don't know the answer to a question that they have, never make something up. Tell them you don't know, but that you'll find somebody who does have the answer and then let them know. I think honesty is the key.

There are some individuals right now at the Division I level who are perceived to be great recruiters, but a lot of people, including prospective players, don't like them. When they get involved in the recruiting process, it starts getting nasty, because all along they've lied to the prospect about what they're going to do and what they can do, and other schools know about it and they let the recruits know about it, too. Someone like that can undo all the good work the other coaches have done.

I think if you're honest with parents, honest with coaches, it will all come back to help you. When I was at Northwestern, we tried to recruit a player who ended up choosing another school. He was a coach's son. The dad pulled me aside and said, "Tim, you know the thing that I really appreciate about you is that you're always honest with me. I always knew where I stood with you. My son always knew where he stood with you."

We didn't get the player; but I really feel like if something happens and his son doesn't work out where he is, I think I'll have a chance to get him, because I was honest about what we could and could not offer him.

Perceptions Count

There's the old saying that perception is reality. How you're perceived in this profession can take you a long way. If you're perceived to be a guy who cuts corners, then pretty soon the reality will be that you can't be trusted. So you should be trying to maintain a high level of honesty at all times. It can only help you.

First impressions count. Before I talk to a player on the phone, I write out the top three or four things that I'm going to talk about. I think the worst thing you can do in making your initial contact with any parent or recruit is not to have an idea of what you're going to talk about. I think the first impression is by far the most important thing and you should be highly organized to make the most of it.

I want to know what a player's weaknesses are, what he thinks his strengths are, and who he feels is going to help him make his decision. I want to know up front if distance is going to be a factor when he is making his decision. Things really seem to go smoothly for me when I pick the phone up and make a phone call knowing what I am going to say; because when the conversation is over, if they think, "Oh, my gosh, this guy didn't know what he was talking about," or "didn't know what he wanted to do," or "didn't have any idea what he was going to do for me or my future," you probably won't get a second chance to make a good first impression. So I think, without a doubt, first impressions are very, very important.

> **"I went to the airport wearing the gorilla suit for one reason – to be remembered."**

Lasting impressions are also made when you meet players for the first time. I once wore a gorilla suit to the airport to meet a player. The player was probably thinking, "This guy's an absolute fool." But, we signed him!

I went to the airport wearing a gorilla suit for one reason. I wanted the guy to remember who I was. I wanted him to remember that when he came and visited this school, Coach Carter came to the airport wearing a gorilla suit. I can tell you, he remembered that first impression. Obviously, some of the these things wouldn't work for you, but don't be afraid to be creative. I think your first impression has to be "stand out" as far as what you're trying to get across to a prospect.

The Mom Factor

I don't care what anybody else tells you. If you don't have mom in your corner, you are in big trouble. I am always concerned when I call a recruit and I can't get his mom on the phone. You talk to dad and dad always talks about, "Well, he's going to make his own decision." That's a bunch of bull. They never make their own decisions. Ever.

What I found out is that I am more successful when I recruit the mother just as hard as I recruit that son. (When recruiting women, it's just the opposite. I have two girls, and if they are recruited, I can guarantee you I'm going to have some serious say in where they go. They're going to listen to me.) So you've got to get on the phone with the mom, and get her on your side.

Before the NCAA outlawed it, I would send little cards to the moms. I'd write a short note on it. "Hope everything's well." "Enjoyed talking with you." "Looking forward to visiting with you when I come in." Then, when I would go to a basketball game (during the time when you couldn't talk to parents), I would have the manager run up in the stands and give her a note. She'd look over and I'd wave.

If you get moms to believe in you, you've won half the battle. Most moms are very affected when their sons leave to go away from home. Dad's the same way. I want to know everything about mom. Where she works. Who her best friend is. Because she's going to tell her best friend what she thinks about you. Very important, the mom's best friend, the dad's best friend. I would even put each parent's best friend on my personal mailing list.

At UNO, when it got down to, say, three positions we were going to be recruiting (hopefully no more than nine guys), every day a coach wrote each one of those players a note. Every day. That may seem impersonal, but that's about as much as you can do now. But with the mom, I wrote her at least two or three notes a week. Find out who her best friend is and write that person a note about your school. Send the best friend a packet about your school. When it comes time for the decisions to be made, if you can develop a relationship with the best friend of the mom or the dad, then you'll have somebody to call and talk to who can give you some information.

Know What You Want – And What Your Boss Wants

> "It was 3 a.m. and I was waiting in an alley for my prospect to come out of a club. That wasn't me."

First, I think you have to know yourself. Don't do things that aren't you. I'll never forget, one time I was in Detroit recruiting a player and I did the stupidest thing I have ever done in my life. I think back on it right now and I get mad at myself for doing it. It was 3:00 in the morning. And I was in an alley. Waiting for my "big-time" prospect to come out of a club.

Now that wasn't me. That was not the environment that I enjoyed being in. We ended up signing the player, but it turned out that he wasn't the right kind of player for us. We released him from his letter of intent before he ever showed up. I had made a mistake. I wasn't being true to myself. I was recruiting a player that I thought would help us win, and I wasn't recruiting a player that I thought fit what I was all about and what my boss was all about. So I wasn't being true to myself.

If you like to have a player who is going to be where he's supposed to be, do what he's supposed to do, and say what he's supposed to say, then you had better recruit that kind of kid. If you don't mind having a guy who talks back to you once in a while, then know that that's important or not important to you when you go out and recruit. Because believe me, you will attract the same kind of player that you are. If you're quiet, you'll attract quiet kids. If you're a loud, rambunctious, do-it-all person, then that's the kind of prospect that you're going to attract.

But you know what I found out is the most important thing? Know what your boss likes. You do all the leg work and sell the player on the school. Then you get your boss involved and he doesn't like the guy. Then you're in trouble. One time, my boss looked at the leg muscles on a player. He liked players with straight up-and-down-looking legs and not the chubby-type legs, because he really felt like he had been successful with those type of players. I thought that was crazy, but it was his decision. We passed on that player, and my former boss won a national championship. So know what your boss likes.

If your boss likes players with great free throw shooting skills and you take him to a situation where a guy's only shooting about 55 percent from the free throw line, or he has a funny shot, you have just set yourself up for defeat. This prospect can't shoot free throws. The player may leave and go some place else and become a small college All-American or second team All Big 10 or Big 12 player. But you have to know what you are looking for in a prospect. Know your environment.

At Northwestern, I couldn't recruit the same type of player that I recruited at Oklahoma State. I tried. I was really good at finding players. I could go out and find a guy that no one knew about who could flat out play. I couldn't do that at Northwestern because academic standards were a lot higher. Schools like Stanford and Vanderbilt were recruiting the same type of player as we were at Northwestern. But when I went out to find those kinds of players and put them in the Chicago environment, they didn't like it.

Other Key Elements

I once recruited a player from rural Alabama. During a weekend in Chicago, we took him down to Michael Jordan's restaurant and as we were driving into downtown Chicago, he looked up and said, "God, it's just like on TV." I was in trouble. The player didn't sign because I took him out of his element. I had tried to bring him some place where he wasn't comfortable. So know your environment, know what a prospect likes and what he doesn't like. Also know your institution.

I used to say that a person can go anywhere and get a quality education. I still believe that. But I don't think you can bring any prospect into your institution and expect him or her to feel comfortable.

Going from Oklahoma State to Northwestern was interesting, because they did

> **"You can lose a recruit if you take him into an uncomfortable situation."**

things so differently at both institutions. At Oklahoma State, we could bring a prospect on campus, show him a good time, have him visit a classroom, and have him visit with an instructor. It was fantastic. No problem.

At Northwestern, the process was just the opposite. When a prospect got on campus, he went through interviews with people who would then tell me whether or not the prospect fit in our system – even though the player had already been admitted. So from that point, you're kind of behind the eight ball. You brought somebody into a situation where others may be thinking that the person won't be successful to begin with.

So really know your school. Know the environment around your school. Are you in an urban situation or are you in a college town? Find out from the prospect and his parents what the needs are *before* you bring him on campus. How important is it that he be near a big city? How important is it that he be able to see the Cubs or the White Sox play? These things may be important to a recruit. Believe me, you can land or lose a recruit simply because you took him into a situation where he wasn't comfortable.

Networking

Another area that is most important to me is networking. Every person, and I mean *every person* that you meet, is important. If there is a custodian in your building, make sure you get to know that person, whoever it is. Some custodians are not from your town and they may know people in a smaller, nearby town. I once landed a recruit from a very, very small town. Believe it or not, our custodian told me about this recruit.

So when I talk about networking, I mean speak to people around you every day. Get to know even the people you don't think can help. They just might be of great help to you. The recruit I mentioned was our leading scorer his first season at Northwestern and we got him because the custodian liked me. So make sure you treat everyone with just as much respect as you do your athletic director.

When networking, I have two lists of people that I send mailings to – administrators and basketball people. I send out something maybe twice a month to people

I've met over the past 10 years. I send things like quotes and stories. Start a mailing list of principals, AAU coaches, basketball junkies, and basketball services.

I make it a point to put on my mailing list those people connected to players I've signed in the past two or three years – the principal, the basketball coach, the AAU coach. You never know when information from a principal may lead you to a good player that nobody has recruited. I keep such people on my personal mailing list for at least three years. They get something from me once or twice a month.

That probably has helped me more than anything else. When I went to a basketball camp, I knew who was working the camp. I'd let them know that I'd be in on a certain night and what I was looking for. I'd ask them to tell me who could play and who couldn't play, because in Division I, I didn't have the time that I used to have for recruiting. I had a certain amount of time in the summer and I had to get on the ball. If I went into a camp looking for players, instead of having somebody already identifying players for me, I was in big trouble.

High school coaches and AAU coaches are working those camps. Get to know them, put them on your list. Send them a mailing once a month. Obviously you can't send coaches shirts or that type of thing, but you know they like stories, quotes. It may not mean a whole lot to you to send something to those guys, but it means a heck of a lot to them that you're thinking about them. It is very worthwhile. Believe me, in two to three years, you'll find that people will be calling you from parts of the country that never called you before, simply because a person that you were really close with knew somebody else and they turned around and called you.

> **"One of the best things you have to offer a player is an environment that meets his needs."**

Teamwork Approach

Don't ever underestimate the importance of having people working for you. When you walk into a camp, you ought to know who is going to work that camp. You ought to know so that when you get there, you can go to them for some information. You want to know who can play and who cannot play. I never went to a camp in the last two years and stayed longer than one day. You'd have coaches staying there two and three days trying to evaluate, trying to lock in. Forget that approach. Find out who can play before you ever get there. And when you get there, the coach will take your card and make sure the player gets it. Don't ever leave a camp without having given a coach a card to give to a player. You've made considerable progress in twenty-four hours, while other recruiters are running around trying to evaluate players.

Principals are very important on your mailing list; otherwise, many times you can't get academic information unless you get it from a coach. A lot of coaches have a lot of power regarding the academic information you receive. You may be calling the coach and saying, "Coach, I need a transcript," and you can't get the transcript. The reason why you can't get the transcript is because the coach is in cahoots with somebody else. If you know the principal of a school, he may go to the computer, pull up a transcript, and you've got the transcript. And you never went through the high school coach. Now, you may think that you shouldn't do things that way; but believe me, you've got to find legal ways to get information. Information is power. If you don't have the information, you have nothing.

Make other assistant coaches your allies. If you know coaches in other conferences, get to know them. These people are also on my mailing list. They receive something from me once a month. Get to know them. If they get in a recruiting war

> **"Lock in on an area and make it work for you. But make sure you take care of those players."**

with a player and the player gets upset at both of them, what happens? They're not going to help you get him. So, say I call Tim up and get Tim involved with this player, I won't have to play against him. I've done it a lot. It has helped and guys have helped me. Make sure you have assistant coaches from other conferences that are your allies. Again, that's part of the networking situation.

Narrow Your Efforts

Focus in on a recruiting area for prospects. Depending on what your budget is, you need to find a part of the country that you go to every year and sign a player. Get to know everybody in that area: the high school coach, AAU coach, the principal, the janitor.

I made it a point that I was going to find players out of the south every year when I was at Oklahoma State. When I went to Northwestern, that helped me. In the state of Georgia, I knew every AAU person. I knew every basketball junkie you could think of in Georgia who amounted to anything. You can do the exact same thing. Lock in on an area and make that area work for you. Then when you get the recruit, you make sure that he can play because you might not be able to go back.

Let's face it, the high school coach always inflates how good a kid is. The AAU coach does the same thing. If you get a player out of this region, you had better make sure he can play. If he goes back and says, "Hey coach, I got a bad deal," you're in trouble. You go back in there and if you haven't taken care of the kid, you won't get a player out of that region anymore.

At UNO, I picked out about four cities within a five- to six-hour radius. I knew anybody that counted in that area. I knew of every basketball player that could play within that area. Any person within that five-hour radius of UNO that met my criteria received information from our staff at least once a month. You don't have to go very far if you know what you're doing. Make that area really work for you.

You should make a serious commitment to being good at what you do. You really have to enjoy what you're doing. For me, it got to the point where, when I locked in on a certain number of players, it was like war. I really enjoyed getting into a recruiting battle with somebody and seeing how I was going to play the part. It was like a game to me. I knew what so-and-so was saying about our program. I knew how the coach felt. I was always trying to piece it all together to make it all come out right. I really enjoyed the hunt.

If you don't enjoy the process, then whatever fire you have right now for recruiting won't matter, because you're not going to stay in this profession very long. If you don't enjoy recruiting, you had better get somebody on your staff who does. You had better find somebody who enjoys getting in the battle, because you won't be in it very long.

> **"Learn all that you can from a mentor – and then do things that help *your* program."**

I really think the days of the so-called great "X-and-O guys," who are able to maintain the high level of excellence in their programs, are becoming a rarity. Players are going where they can play. Players are going where they like a certain brand of basketball, and where they like the coach, or where they like the assistant or staff.

If a player can't see the fire and passion in you as a coach, then I think you're in trouble. So *enjoy* getting involved with trying to find recruits.

Don't Try and Re-Invent the Wheel

As a coach, you should have a mentor. This was very important to me. George Raveling has meant so much to me in this profession, because he's the absolute best at every aspect of college basketball. He's a great salesman. He's a good coach. He's a great recruiter. He's somebody I can trust. Find someone you really respect and learn everything you can from them about recruiting.

Not everything that has been done will work for you. You've got to find out what is best for your program. Find somebody in the profession who you can look up to and that you respect. Get to know them and "steal" everything you can from them. Tell them that you respect them and that you want to know everything that makes them good – how to do this, how to do that. But remember, this person needs to be and have the same type of moral values that you have. Find somebody you can learn from. It will really help you.

In recruiting, you must lower the number of recruiting prospects as quickly as possible, rather than having a huge list to contend with. You've got to make it personal. So get your numbers down as quickly as possible. By the middle of August, if we don't have the recruits down to a workable number, so I will be able to write those personal notes, then I'm fooling myself. If you're head coach, make your assistant coaches cut it. If you're an assistant coach, head coaches don't want to be fooling around calling 75 prospects.

Prospects can tell immediately if it is just a routine phone call. Get your numbers down so you can get to know the players. The coach needs to be able to say, "How's your mom doing? How's Larry doing? How's your little brother John doing?" If you can't say that after about three phone calls, then you haven't done your job. You have too many people on your list.

> **If at first you don't succeed, try again with someone else.**

When you are recruiting and you go to a game, don't just sit there. Work the crowd. How many times have you gone to a game and you've seen coaches lined up behind the basket? What they're trying to do is make sure that the player sees them. The rule now allows you to go into the stands and say hello to the parents and visit with them. I think it's both a good and a bad rule, because you've got idiots out there who go and sit by parents the whole game. In many cases that eliminates that school from contention, because you start to annoy the parents.

Move around and work the crowd. Ask questions. Find out if the player is a decent human being. You don't have the time that you used to have in recruiting. If you're standing up behind the basket so a player can see you, then you've just helped me. While you're there, I'm collecting information left and right, trying to find out as much about the player as I can. Work the crowd; it's very important.

How often have you gone into a gym and spent a lot of time working the head coach, but you didn't end up with any information? You walked out feeling that you had wasted an afternoon. In that kind of situation, get to know the assistant coach. Get to know the manager. Get to know as many people who don't get all of attention as you can possibly get to know. They'll give you all the information you need. They're just happy to talk to you. They will give you a feel for the prospect and whether or not the prospect has potential for your program.

Get to know people like that because you can cut your losses and get out a lot sooner than dealing with the head coach. For example, if you know that Notre Dame is recruiting a player, that can change the way you look at a prospect and provide helpful insight into your chances.

Set-Up and Close

When you go into a home, if a parent offers you anything, take it. You don't want to offend anybody. If you're a head coach, make sure you tell your assistant coach what to expect. Make sure when you go into a home that you have a good idea what you're going to do and what you're not going to do, because you can make the deal or you can lose the deal just by not knowing what's going on when you go into a home.

A while back, I was recruiting in Michigan. I had found a point guard that I was interested in. He could play and was a great kid. I was in there every week working the kid. I got to know his coach. I got to know everybody. September rolled around. I wasn't aware that the state of Michigan has a rule that the coach cannot be in the gym with more than three players. I took my head coach up there.

We found out that the player could only work out with two others in the gym. He was a point guard and you obviously want the head coach to see all of what he could in the open floor, his decision-making, his shooting, and his ball handling. I took my head coach into an environment that did not allow the player to shine. It was my fault. We lost him. Not because the player didn't want to come to our school, but because my boss didn't like what he saw. So if you're going to close a deal as an assistant, you had better make sure that you allow your boss to see the kid play his absolute best. If he doesn't, it's your fault.

As a head coach, tell your people that when they take you to see a recruit to make sure it is the best environment possible, so that you can make an informed decision. We lost that player because the head coach didn't want to take him. But he made a decision without having all the information.

I feel badly because the high school coach was probably the most respected high school coach in the state of Michigan. He had virtually delivered the player to me. He wouldn't let anybody else talk to him. And because of my mistake, I lost a shot at signing a very good player. It took me an entire year to mend my relationship with that coach. I wanted to be able to go back up there and recruit again.

> **"It's not over when the prospect doesn't sign. You might get him next week or next year."**

You *can* use your relationship with a player to get him or her to come your way. If they like you, use it. There may be something about your school that they may not like, but don't start rationalizing as to why you can't get them. Let him or her make the decision – don't make it yourself. But do use your relationship to close the deal, if you can.

Sign on the Dotted Line...

When it gets down to closing the deal, I always tell myself, "Be a friend, not a recruiter." When you find out it's between you and another school, you might find they don't really want to talk to you in the first place. They're uptight. Mom's on their case, Dad's on them, their brother's on them, the coach is on them to make a decision. So when you call them to close the deal, or if it's getting close to that point, be a friend. Don't even talk about recruiting.

Never negative recruit. Everybody in coaching understands what that does to you. If you can't sign a player based on how good you are, based on how good your institution is, based on how good your head coach is, then it does you no good to negative recruit.

If the player happens to tell the coach where he decides to go what you said, you have possibly lost a friend. You haven't maintained that networking situation. Again, I'm not saying when it gets down to decision time that you don't hammer away. When you know it's over, thank the player and thank his parents. Drop them a note. Drop the coach a note. Wish the player well, because you might get him or her next year, or in a week, or two years later. At least you haven't hurt yourself as far as the big picture is concerned, and that big picture, in my opinion, is your network and your allies.

> **"Whether the high school coach is on your side or not, let him or her know what is going on."**

Keep the high school coach informed. Whether the coach is on your side or not, let him or her know what's going on. They're either going to hurt you or they're going to help you. If you know a high school coach is hurting you, and you let them know what you're doing, you at least have an idea of what they're doing because they're going to give you some information.

High school coaches have egos and they want them stroked. They want to feel like they are making a great impact on their player's life and they want to feel like they're having a say in what they do. So keep them informed as to what's going on.

Stand Out From the Crowd

If you are in the hunt, but you feel that your prospect has started to lean the other way, do something different. If you're writing him three notes a day, write him eight notes a day. That exact tactic might not work, but you have to do something. When it gets down to that point, everybody's pretty much doing the same thing. If you have the budget, send something priority mail.

Two years ago, I got to the point where I started sending out priority mail once a week: "Larry, you are our number one priority." It's less expensive than FedEx, but you're still being different. Branch out. You may have to start working somebody else in the prospect's network. You may have to start working an assistant. But you've got to find a different angle at that point.

I never stop until the prospect tells me they are going somewhere else – or until they actually sign with someone else. Until they tell me, "Coach, I'm 100% sure that I'm going here." I think you have to keep fighting. Because you never know what might happen in the meantime. It's like someone being in a coma. You never know what brings them out.

Quality Players

I have a rule. I never recruit anybody that I can't leave at home with my family if I'm gone. If I'm recruiting somebody that I feel questionable about, because I want my players to come over to my house, if I felt like I couldn't trust this person with my family, I got out. I didn't even think twice about it. Not all young men and women are private school candidates. But I think that's where you have to get to know somebody who knows them as a person.

There are no *secrets* to becoming a top recruiter. But there are definitely guidelines that you can use to help yourself succeed.

Author Profile: Tim Carter

Tim Carter is the head men's basketball coach at the University of Texas-San Antonio. Highly regarded as one of the top recruiters in the country for 15 years, the former Kansas University graduate has had coaching stops at the University of Oklahoma, Midwestern State University, University of Houston, Oklahoma State University, Northwestern University and the University of Nebraska at Omaha.

HOW TO RECRUIT EFFECTIVELY WITHOUT SCHOLARSHIPS

A Panel with Teri Clemens, Bob Nielson and Dan Smith

Q: *All of you have been very successful in building and maintaining competitive Division III athletic programs because you are strong believers in the Division III concept. What aspect of Division III athletics got you hooked in the first place and what elements have kept you thriving in Division III?*

Bob Nielson: If I had to summarize why I've enjoyed my association with Division III, I'd use the word "balance." I think Division III represents a high degree of balance in terms of coaching. I've had opportunities to be involved not just in football, but in athletics in general as well as administrative decisions made by the college. My background includes being a director of admissions and also, before the NCAA changed the rules, a director of financial aid. I enjoyed being involved in the decisions that affect enrollment at the institution.

I'm also a member of the faculty. I enjoy teaching in the classroom. Division III also seems to attract athletes who have a broader perspective. They tend to be more interested in a combination of academics, athletics and a social environment than someone in a scholarship program. These things make the life of a Division III coach very exciting and very fulfilling.

Teri Clemens: I can honestly say the division of the school had no impact on my taking a position at Washington at all. I was a high school coach and was offered a position at the University of Kentucky and at Washington University, a Division III school, on the same day. I took the position at Washington University, mostly because it was just completing a beautiful athletic complex and it had a super athletic director. I believed I had a future there. I believed we could win there.

I tell the athletes that we recruit, "It's the same gold that you put on your finger whether you're in Division III or Division I if you win the national title." The division meant nothing to me. I still recruit with the philosophy that it's the *class* of the program and not the *division* of the program. It just does not matter to me.

To this day, I can say that I have found balance as well. I was not a mother of six before I went to Washington University. I couldn't imagine being a mother and saying, "I need another challenge, so I think I'll be a collegiate coach." But I became a collegiate coach and then found that I absolutely had enough balance in my life that I could be a mother of six, too.

Dan Smith: My original desire to coach at the Division III level was probably more selfish than any other reason. With a Ph.D. and a strong coaching background, I wanted to have a tenured faculty position, as well as be head basketball coach, and I couldn't do that at a Division I or Division II school, because if you're coaching, they are usually not going to allow you to be in a tenure-track faculty position.

> **"In Division I, if you are coaching, they are not usually going to let you be on a tenure-track."**

Balance is important. When I was at Illinois as an assistant basketball coach, probably half of the players at that level honestly thought when they came in that they were going to play in the NBA.

At Brockport, I don't think any of my players ever came in thinking that they were going to play in the NBA. In a way, that's an advantage and in a way, it's a disadvantage.

Q: *All of you are firm believers in utilizing the entire campus community in the recruiting process. Which departments and individuals on campus do you believe are critical components in recruiting?*

Teri Clemens: I think that most people would immediately say admissions and financial aid. At our particular institution, we almost shy away from visiting those two departments. We have no say as to who gets into the university and what kind of financial aid package they have. Instead, we tend to work a lot with the post-placement department, the career department. We use it to show recruits what a great place it is to graduate from because of what they can do after their university days.

One of the best examples I can give is the year we had four seniors who won a national title and one of them received a full four-year scholarship to medical school at Washington University valued at $130,000. The second one landed an accounting position that started at a salary of $44,000. The third one is an engineer who started at $48,000 and the fourth one received a scholarship to occupational therapy school. We have great success stories and that's what we try to utilize.

We can go to the post-placement department and they can tell the students about the great things that can come their way, and they can talk to seniors and graduates who have been successful.

Dan Smith: I think the academic department is critical. One thing I say to every recruit is, "You're only going to have basketball for four years, but you're going to have a degree for the rest of your life." So you need to make sure that you help them do everything they can to get the best education possible. So I work with the academic department a lot.

Bob Nielson: At our level, athletic recruiting is an institutional process.

Teamwork is critical to our success. The admissions people can be very helpful. At Wartburg, we had a talented woman in the admissions office who coordinated visits for us. In football, we had between 200 and 250 visitors a year. If I had to coordinate all of those visits, it would have taken a tremendous amount of my time. So I worked with her to coordinate the visits. She knew the faculty. I sat down with her and gave her an indication of which faculty I'd like the recruits to visit with. She had a group of tour guides available to her that were student-trained. She arranged tours as a part of these visits. That was extremely helpful to us.

One of the most important things for a coach to do is to get around and meet as many people on campus as you can. You need to seek out people who can be helpful in your recruiting. When I was at Ripon College, one of the people that I met in the first couple of weeks was the person who directed the food service. He came up to me and said, "Coach, any time you bring a parent or family on campus, I'd like to visit with them."

> **"One of the most important things to do is to get out and meet as many people on campus as you can."**

So I'd take the family over to the cafeteria for lunch and he'd come sit at our table. He would talk about the meal plan. The parents thought that was very, very important. They wanted to know that their son or daughter was going to be fed well. Whether they could get seconds free or if they were going to have to pay for them was important to athletes.

If your administration has an interest in athletic recruiting, there are times when a recruit might be able to talk with the president or one of your academic deans or vice presidents. When you have a student-athlete on campus and a member of the administration stops by to say, "Hi," that can make a great impression with the family and with the student-athlete.

We talk a lot in recruiting about building relationships, and there's no better way to help a student-athlete build a relationship with your campus than to have them meet as many people as possible. The more help that you can get from other departments on campus, the more successful you're going to be.

Q: *How do you identify your talent pool and what do you consider your best selling point to potential recruits?*

Dan Smith: When identifying a talent pool, the key variable is need. You have to decide exactly what the needs of your program are. In Division III, sometimes that varies. Your players don't necessarily tell you that they are planning on quitting or transferring. On a whim, they could leave practice and you might not ever see them again. Then, as far as selling points, you need to decide what makes you unique. Every program has at least one unique aspect. One unique thing about me is that I am part of the academic faculty and I have a Ph.D. They don't necessarily make your program any better, but they are still unique things. Think through what makes you unique and use that in the recruiting process.

Bob Nielson: Identifying the talent pool is one of the easiest tasks for coaches because of the available resources. Scouting services are as helpful for Division III programs as they are for all the other levels. You can ask for specific states and specific grade point averages with many of these services. You can select out a group of prospects that is a pretty good match with your institution to start with.

> **"It's critical to narrow down your talent pool to a smaller group."**

Your admissions office is going to be a great source of names. Most college admissions offices start the year with anywhere from 20,000 to 30,000 student names. You can coordinate the information that you have with the information that they have to find home addresses and telephone numbers for prospects you know are good players. It will save you some time instead of collecting that information yourself.

It's critical to refine your talent pool to a group that you can work with. That's really the most important phase of recruiting. In Iowa, for example, there are roughly 400 high schools. Let's say that each one of those schools has two college football prospects, which would be a very conservative number. That's 800 high school football prospects. Last year, Division I schools around the country signed less than 20 of those players on scholarships. There's a tremendous pool left.

How can you find the ones that best fit your institution? You have to start early. I do a lot of my screening work in the summer. I spend a tremendous amount of time on telephone and mail campaigns to try to identify those students that fit us best. I picked up at least one thing from the business world. It has to do with "problem" and "need." All the prospects that we work with have a problem — that problem is what school they're going to choose. The question is what their need is. What are they really looking for?

If we run into somebody in our early recruiting who needs to have an athletic scholarship, and that's their number one priority in choosing a school, that's somebody who's not going to be worth much time recruiting. But if we find somebody whose need is to get a good education and to be a part of a quality football program, that's somebody that we feel we have a good match with. That elevates them to "top prospect" status.

You can use your screening process to save you time and help you identify people within the talent pool who are prospects that you should be focusing your efforts on.

Teri Clemens: Although Washington University is considered to be a fairly wealthy institution, the money doesn't always come my way. We don't have a lot of money for scouting services to identify prospects. Our admissions department asks prospective students if they're interested in any sports and then they give us a list. That gives us a starting point. That gives us what I cautiously call "filler athletes."

The impact players are those who I go out and find myself. We spend a lot of time watching videotapes, because it's cheap. We evaluated 124 videotapes this year and three of those athletes are coming to Washington University. With a team of 12 in volleyball, that's what we were looking for.

We recruit "position-specific" and we look for the traits that we need in players. We are specific about what we're looking for, whether that's a leader who's a middle blocker or a really rowdy, spirited, emotional kind of kid. We share that with them. We never negatively recruit. We try to emphasize our strengths, thinking that if they're looking at us in the first place, we have a chance to get them.

We take a personal touch. We believe in attention to detail. So we make their visit as attentive as we can and we make sure that they get a personalized agenda before they arrive for a campus visit. We have a thank you note in the mail before they even arrive home a lot of times. We touch on a lot of personal things. In our building, we have a little area where we invite students to sit down with their parents and we have pictures all over the wall. It's our little volleyball archive. A lot of personalization, that's what we can offer them.

Q: *In evaluation of talent, what is your system for mailing, for phone calls, and for videotape evaluation and how much do you do with that?*

Dan Smith: We separate it into an "A" pool and "B" pool. The "A" pool, I'm going to call every other week. The "B" pool, I'm going to phone once a month. We prioritize our contacts. As far as keeping prospects posted by mail, I send them pertinent information, but I don't send them junk.

I don't want to send out things that they don't even look at. So I try to determine whether this is something that will benefit them, something they will utilize, something they're interested in. But I don't send them things just to be sending them things.

Bob Nielson: We use what I call an "interactive mail system" which generates specific mailings in response to what the student-athlete does. We send out a letter with a questionnaire. If they return the questionnaire, they get a letter in response to that. If after a month they don't return the questionnaire, they get another letter. It's all done on the computer. If you have someone at your institution who knows computers, they can help you devise your own system.

> **"We rely more on high school coaches than we do on videotapes."**

When the student-athlete makes an application for admission, we get that information from the admissions office and that triggers another specific mailing. We have separate mailings that go out at specific times to reinforce certain aspects that we think are important in the recruiting process; things that are happening within our program.

I think the telephone is a great instrument in terms of recruiting. I think the key time to phone is early. We try to contact every good prospect that we have in our files personally by phone in the months of June and July. It makes for a shorter summer, but that is one time during the year when Division III prospects aren't getting bombarded by phone calls. Not every coach is working over the summer to the same degree. So you can be one of the first to get a personal contact and maybe encourage an early campus visit.

When it comes to videotape, I would honestly say that we probably rely more on high school coaches in terms of their evaluation than we do on videotape. But there's only myself and two other members of our staff that recruit. We get out to see a lot of high school games and we try to see people personally. But if someone wants to send us a videotape, we always say yes and we'll look at it. We'll always send a follow-up note both to the coach and to the athlete after we've seen the videotape. We have to rely on coaches that know our program and know their athletes to get a good feel for the type of young man who can contribute here.

Teri Clemens: We recruit nationwide, and because of our lack of recruiting money, the videotape has been a big part of the process. It also can be really deceptive. If they put a lot of money in it to make a professional videotape, they can make themselves look pretty darn good. We've been fooled a couple of times by that.

We send an evaluation to the recruit afterward. It's a personalized form. We comment on each skill that they show on the tape, and we write some notes about where we think they are now and what we can do. We try to keep it really positive. We don't rip them apart. We do let them know if we think they could fit into our program and how we see them fitting in.

If we think they can be an impact player, we let them know that right away because, hey, everybody wants to start. We're really good about sending personal notes. If we send an original questionnaire and don't get a response, two weeks later we send a personal letter saying, "We really want to hear from you."

I'm writing letters constantly. I write at least 10 a day that are just a couple of lines long. It makes a big difference.

We get our athletes involved. Recruits tell us that this is the most special thing they ever got from us. During the season, we have each one of our athletes write down just a sentence or two on one topic. We'll say, "Mary, you write a sentence on our team travel." "Julie, you write a sentence on what it's like to stay in a motel with this crew." We write about our meals on the road, our practices, etc. Then we'll format it. They can read a sentence or two from players much more rapidly, much more eagerly, than they would from coaches. And, needless to say, we get a lot of positive feedback on that. When they come to campus to visit, they always have something to say about the things they've read. It's been one of the best things we've ever done.

Q: *How actively do you involve your players and other students on campus in the recruiting process? What guidelines have you established when it comes to utilizing students in the recruiting process?*

Bob Nielson: Our students are our best ambassadors of our program and our school. Anytime a student-athlete visits our campus, they spend time with our student-athletes. At Wartburg, most of our student-athletes came from the state of Iowa. If they were within driving distance, they would come up for a day. If they came in the morning, we made sure that they got some time over lunch to spend with one of our student-athletes. We might have even tried to find somebody who didn't have to go to class right away after lunch so that they could take them over to the residence hall, show them around their room and introduce them to other people.

> "Our students are our best ambassadors."

We also have our student-athletes make contacts when they go home over break. If there's somebody that we're recruiting from their local area, we might have them try to see the recruit over break. We have them let the prospect know that we're glad that they are considering our college.

It's a situation where if you have people that are very satisfied in your program, they're going to be a tremendous asset in your recruiting.

Teri Clemens: Our students are very involved in the recruiting process. We always have a luncheon when a recruit comes on campus. It's not mandatory by any means, but the word gets out. They really enjoy it, especially when it's non-season, because it's a time for them to get together, too. It's great for the team camaraderie, and it's a chance for recruits to see the team together. One of the best things about our team is the camaraderie and the closeness of the players.

Q: *What do you tell recruits are the advantages of playing Division III as opposed to Division II or Division I?*

Teri Clemens: I try not to isolate us as being different in a world of competition. The greatest asset we may have is the balance that we can offer.

The best example I can give is that we've had a couple of Division I transfers in the past few years. One of them was a national player of the year, so we were pretty fortunate. The reason that she came back to us was because she remembered us talking about what a great balance Washington had and she didn't feel the experience she was having was very balanced.

She was up at 5:00 a.m. in the weight room every morning. She was very academically-oriented, but wasn't getting to take the courses that she needed because she needed to be done by 1:00 p.m. to get to practice. She remembered it being different at our institution and so she came back to us.

We talk about balance, but we certainly don't talk about the differences between us and the other divisions because there is no difference when it comes to competition. I know that our athletes want to win every bit as much as anybody else.

Dan Smith: I think we have an advantage in two areas – less rules and less pressure. When I went from Illinois to Brockport, I couldn't believe I didn't have to worry about a recruiting calendar. I remember the very first tournament that I went to was an All-Star tournament. I was with a friend of mine who was a Division II coach. We were both interested in the same guy and knew we were going to be recruiting against each other. I walked right down and talked to the guy. He couldn't, because he had calendar restrictions; he couldn't talk to that guy at that time. That could be an advantage.

> **"Overall, there is less pressure at Division III than at Division I."**

As far as the pressure on the players, it's a little bit different as well. For example, one year when I was at Illinois, we had a player on the free throw line with two seconds left on the clock. We were down by one point, the game was on national TV and the Big 10 title was on the line.

We don't have quite that same amount of pressure at Brockport. Granted, pressure is a perception. Consequently, if an individual perceives that a free throw is that important, it could be the same. But I think overall there is less pressure at Division III than at Division I.

Bob Nielson: We try to focus on education as an advantage. We feel that a student-athlete in our program is going to have more time to commit to their education than they might at a scholarship-level school.

We also emphasize the fact that they're going to graduate in four years, because over 90 percent of our students, and well over 90 percent of our athletes, do. That's something in a day and age when college is more and more expensive.

We don't redshirt in our league. For the highly-talented student-athlete, that means they're going to be able to come in and play sooner than they might at a Division I or Division II program. That's very important to some people. They don't want to wait two or three years to have a chance to play.

> **"Our athletes don't have to wait two or three years to play."**

Q: *Has the tightening of recruiting regulations for Division I and Division II helped Division III athletics? In what way has it affected your program in particular?*

Dan Smith: First, the recruiting calendar. Second, financial aid. I was astounded to find out when I went from Division I to Division III that if I had a prospect who was eligible for financial aid at Division III, he could receive more money than we could have given him with a basketball scholarship at Division I.

Bob Nielson: The recruiting restrictions in Divisions I and II provide an opportunity for Division III coaches to be more persistent and more consistent, which is something that is preferred in terms of personal contacts.

If you're in a situation where you can do home visits, you can be out on the road at times when there are dead periods for Division I and II. You can be there on a regular basis throughout the course of the time in which a student-athlete is making a decision.

For example, we had a young man one year who was listed as one of the top five football players in the state of Iowa. Because of the recruiting calendar, I was able to make three home visits to see him. Fortunately, he lived fairly close to the town in which the school was located, so it wasn't a significant drive. The parents were very impressed by the fact that the head football coach was in the home three different times and none of the other schools (scholarship schools) made that kind of a commitment. You have an opportunity because of the limit on rules to be consistent and persistent in your approach.

Q: *In summary, what are the most important things to remember about recruiting effectively without scholarships?*

Bob Nielson: The first thing is to be the most knowledgeable person on campus. I find it amazing to talk with friends of mine who are coaches who know very little about what's happening in other areas of their institution.

Whether you want it to be or not, in the recruiting process, you become the contact for that student-athlete and the family, not just for football or basketball or volleyball, or whatever the sport may be, but for the institution.

So you need to know what's happening in the academic areas as well. That means you have to get out and talk with faculty, take an active interest in their programs and go to some of the other events on campus. You have to know what students do for fun. If you're out of touch with that, it makes it difficult to talk about campus environment and social activities when students and parents ask about that.

Know what's going on in your school's other athletic programs. We get a tremendous number of dual-sport athletes in Division III at our institution. So I want to be aware of what other coaches are doing.

You have to know admissions procedures. How to apply, and what forms they need. You have to know how to apply for financial aid. There are specifics you can and can't do with financial aid. If you know the procedures, and if you know how to apply for it, you can help the family through that process and build very strong relationships with them. You need to know about housing on campus and registration. There are just so many areas that relate to the recruiting process that you have to be "an expert" in. If you get a question that you can't answer, at least be a resource to get that question answered for them.

> **"Plan how you will screen out your prospects."**

Second, have a recruiting plan. I talk with other coaches about their recruiting plans and some do a much better job with organization than I do. Others don't have a plan at all. They say they make a few calls here, write a letter here. That's not a plan in terms of how you are going to identify prospects. You need to plan how you will screen those prospects down; take that pool of over 1,000 people that we usually start the year with, and try to get to a pool of 200 to 300 that we really think are good fits for our institution.

The third stage is taking that group and building relationships with them. Division III recruiting is like a big funnel. You have to have enough people to go in at the top that enough come out at the bottom. The way that happens is by building a relationship that sells them on the opportunities that your school has and how that meets their needs. Involve the entire college in the screening process. That can multiply your efforts as a recruiter. Start early and be organized. And get out of the blocks a little bit quicker and get a leg up on your competition.

Teri Clemens: Communication may be the biggest difference in recruiting without scholarships. We try to be as personable as we can because it doesn't cost any money. It's the intangibles. I remember that I had a recruit in my office several years ago. Her name was Nikki. I said, "Nikki, one of the best things that we can offer you at

Washington University is we can help you to be an independent woman of the 90s. When you graduate from Washington University in four years, you're going to feel like you've achieved independence."

I asked her, "Do you think you're independent now?" She said, "Yeah, I'm independent. I think I'm pretty independent. Dad, do you think I'm independent?"

The point is, we can fill those intangibles. We can help you to develop as a person. We're still promoting some of those old-fashioned traits at Washington. In general, we just think you can be a better player because you played for us, and we think that you can be a better person because you attended Washington University.

We have a list on our wall that we call our "Givens." We think it's a given at Washington University that you're going to get a good academic education, so we don't have to promote it.

We think it's a given that you're going to graduate in four years; everyone has who has entered our program. We think it's a given that you're going to graduate. I am tickled when people ask me what our graduate percentages are. It's 100%. We've never had anybody not graduate.

> "We think it's a given that you are going to graduate; everyone else has."

It's a given that we have a beautiful campus; you're going to enjoy your walk around campus. It's a given that you're going to laugh during your campus visit. I think it's a really good idea to put a list of "Givens" up, even if it's just a reminder to you during a visit, because we all have givens. So while you're visiting with parents and students, you can constantly refer to your list of "Givens" on the wall.

We like to challenge the students we recruit and we don't like to go after "just the Division III athletes." I'm often offended by scouting reports that say a player is "Division I" or "Division III." While those offend me, I can also tell athletes that they'll be challenged throughout the year and if they're at an elite level at Washington, we'll find other challenges for them. They can try out at elite levels and we have had players in the Olympic festival.

Finally, we try to maintain a program, not just a team. When I first started out, I recruited a team. I just wanted six recruits that first year and I just wanted the best athletes I could get. I was so exhausted at the end of the season that I took a year off. We rested on our laurels. Then we paid for it the following year.

So now we have a recruiting *program* and every year I want to get one impact player and support staff. We've become pretty good at that and it's been a real strength of ours. We explain to our team that we've built a *program* at Washington, and they can appreciate that.

They love being a part of that and their expectations have become higher.

Dan Smith: Gather as much information as possible. You not only need to have physiological information and skill information, you also need psychological information. Granted, as a sports psychologist, I certainly have a bias toward this area.

> **"Collect basic psychological information as well as skill-based information."**

There are ways that you can gather psychological information. You would never think of recruiting an individual that you didn't know a lot about his/her skill level or cardiovascular fitness. You should at least collect some basic psychological information.

You need to be creative. We didn't have to be creative at Illinois. We really didn't have any budget restrictions. Essentially, we got whatever we needed, as far as recruiting went. Then I went to Division III and had absolutely no recruiting budget my first year. That's a difference of night and day. I volunteered to observe student teachers in Long Island so I could get a couple of Long Island trips paid for every semester. I think you need to be creative in how to fund your recruiting at Division III.

I think another critical element is identifying only those individuals that meet your admission standards. Don't waste time on the individuals that aren't admissible. I think too many times as coaches we get so excited about a player, we see him or her play and then we decide we're interested in recruiting that person right away. Maybe they're not admissible; don't waste your time. Find out about whether they're admissible as soon as possible.

Find out who is going to help make the decision. I think that's another critical point. There are different people in different roles who are going to have influence on that student-athlete. And it's drastically different. Sometimes the high school coach will be the critical person who is going to help make the decision. Sometimes the high school coach will have absolutely no say in the decision whatsoever. And it's critical that you, as a recruiter, are able to read this situation very quickly. Finally, be able to adapt quickly as well.

One year, I was recruiting twins from Long Island. I was really interested in one of them, but they were twins. How do you recruit one and not the other? I thought the other twin could be a decent player, but I didn't know how much he was going to play right off the bat. It just shows how many errors you make in recruiting. I went into the home and recruited them both because I thought that if the one twin goes, the other twin would follow. But I could tell that the better player of the two was thinking he was going to get a scholarship offer from another school, so he wasn't as interested.

The other one, however, was very interested. On the phone the next few weeks after that, it was the second twin who would always talk to me. It wasn't the one that I really wanted. What ended up happening was they both ended up coming.

The one I initially wanted never did get the scholarship he wanted. At the last minute, he said that he was going to come. So I ended up getting both the twin brothers. The one that I didn't think was as good started for me as a freshman. He started for four years. The other one ended up being a good player, just like I'd anticipated, and both of them made All-American. So you have to make sure that you read the situation. It's critical.

Bob Nielson: The key to successful recruiting is recruiting across divisions. Whether you are recruiting with scholarships or without scholarships, you need to work to build a relationship with the student-athlete and represent your institution well. As a coach in a non-scholarship program, you cannot see the inability to offer a scholarship as a negative.

If you see it as a negative, the student-athletes are going to see it as a negative and they're not going to feel good about what you're saying about your program. We never talk about the fact that we're a non-scholarship school.

We say that we're Division III and that doesn't mean we're third class; we think we have a first-class program that emphasizes a good balance between academics and athletics.

> **"If you see Division III as a negative, so will your recruits."**

Teri Clemens: As coaches, we sometimes forget one of the greatest things that we have to promote is ourselves. Oftentimes student-athletes choose your institution because of you. We need to know our own strengths as people and what we have to offer. We can't just study the strengths of our universities and colleges, but also know ourselves.

We also need to work on self-improvement, whether in recruiting, in administration, or in coaching tactics. It took me a long time to realize that was an invaluable tool that we should share with recruits. They like to know that we're trying to get better, too. They know that we're going to be better coaches if we continue to go to clinics and conventions and recruiting seminars.

It's also essential that we are either creative in designing our own programs and implementing our own tools, or that we are innovative, meaning that we can implement someone else's plan and adapt it to our own program.

Not everyone has creative juices, but everybody can at least recognize a good idea, realize that it wouldn't work exactly in their program, but if they can shift it a little bit, it can work. I can't call somebody every week because we can't afford it, but I can call them one week and drop them a note the next. We can all be innovative and adapt situations to our own programs and be successful. There's no excuse why a coach can't get the players he or she wants and needs, just by being more creative or innovative.

Dan Smith: You need to know your financial aid situation. You need to really be an expert on financial aid at your university, because you don't have scholarships. Also, know what others are offering.

I remember recruiting a young man who was telling me about another Division III school in the area (a private, very expensive school) that was recruiting him. The tuition there was $16,000 a year and he said that they were going to give him part of that in a scholarship. I knew it wasn't a scholarship because they were a Division III school. Obviously, they don't have scholarships, but they found some way to give him some aid. He said, "They're going to give me $10,000 in aid for a year."

So I did the math really quickly in my head and figured that meant he was going to pay $6,000 a year. Then I said to him, "Do you realize that our tuition for an entire year is $3,000? So even with $10,000, you're still $3,000 behind?" You need to know what your situation is.

Know what advantages you have. If you're a state school, especially at a Division III level, you have some big advantages because of costs. Don't give up when the individual tells you that they're going to wait and receive a scholarship. Don't give up until he signs a letter of intent. All along, you should be saying, "It would be nice if you got a Division I scholarship and I'd be really happy for you. It would be the best thing and I would encourage you to take it. But if you don't, we're still interested in you." So don't give up if they say they're going to get a scholarship.

Finally, don't believe that Division III means lower quality because it doesn't necessarily mean lower quality.

Panel Profile:

   Teri Clemens is the head volleyball coach at Washington (MO) University. She has been named NCAA Division III Coach-of-the-Year five times and is a 10-time Conference Coach-of-the-Year award winner. Her Bears teams have won seven Division III national championships and her teams have won 87 percent of their matches.

   Bob Nielson is the head football coach and associate athletics director at the University of Wisconsin-Eau Claire. A Coach-of-the-Year award winner, he has 10 years of college recruiting experience. A graduate of Wartburg (IA) College, other coaching stops include Ripon (WI) College and his alma mater. Bob has led his teams to post-season NCAA Division III playoffs.

   Dan Smith has over 10 years of college recruiting experience on the NAIA, Division I and Division III levels. His coaching stops include Brigham Young University-Hawaii, the University of Illinois-Champaign and the State University of New York-Brockport. The former men's basketball coach is currently associate professor of physical education at SUNY-Brockport.

TEAMWORK IN RECRUITING: WORKING WITH YOUR ADMISSIONS OFFICE

by Dave Davis

I spent 25 years in the Navy, and graduated from the Naval Academy. In the 70's, the Navy had tremendous retention problems. We were really pressed from the top down to retain the best sailors. I guess that's where I first developed my philosophy of trying to always press the edge of the envelope. In the Navy, you really have to abide by the rules – but it doesn't say you can't press the edge of the envelope. We were pressured to keep the best sailors in the Navy because they were going out of the service in droves.

One of the first things I tried to learn was the detailing system. That's the assignment system the Navy uses. I felt it was important to learn how it worked and how I could best utilize it to my advantage. To give you an example, we had a young man we were trying hard to retain. He was working as a boiler technician. It's an unenviable job which involves working in a hot, sweaty, steamy boiler room. The boiler technicians oversee the boiling of water to make the steam that's used to propel the ship. This particular sailor was a fantastic leader. He was also an all-around good person and the kind of sailor we needed in the Navy.

But he wasn't interested in being a boiler technician and he wasn't interested in staying in the Navy very long. But one day he told me, "If you get me shore duty in Brooklyn, I'll stay in the Navy."

That would prove to be quite a challenge. There aren't any Navy ships and boilers in Brooklyn. But I didn't give up. I looked around, did some homework, and made a few calls. I found a Naval Reserve Center in Brooklyn that had an opening for a librarian. In the Navy, jobs are set up by what your rating is or by what your field of specialization is. This particular opening was designed for an operations specialist – someone who's used to managing complicated tasks and dealing with confidential and classified information.

But I wasn't deterred. I called the Reserve Center and asked how long the position had been open. They said, "Three years. We can never get anybody here." I said, "Would you take a boiler technician?"

"We would take anybody to do this job," the person in Brooklyn said. But it's not that easy getting a sailor transferred in the Navy. I called Washington and, using "the gift of gab" that's so important in things like this, I tried to make a deal. I said, "I've got a super sailor that will stay in the Navy if you'll give him this job in Brooklyn."

And what was their reply? "He's not an operations specialist."

But I pressed on and to make a long story short, the transfer went through. The former boiler room technician not only stayed in the Navy but he served in Brooklyn for three years and reached the rank of Chief Petty Officer. He wrote me a letter five or six years ago, thanking me for helping him out. That's just one example of what can be accomplished if you push the envelope.

Admissions Directors

Admissions directors are becoming a lot like head coaches. They're expendable if they don't win. Admissions directors who don't bring in enough paying students to keep the ivy on the walls are being asked to leave. And many of them have been at their school for 14, 15 or 16 years. Admissions directors are really in the same business that you're in. By working together with them, you can help each other out.

At most schools, "diversity" is a very important word when it comes to admissions. There's a tremendous amount of pressure on the admissions department to create diversity at a school. Whether it means getting the drummer, the trombone player, the African-American or the super person with the 1600 SAT score, a school needs good diversity to make a good student body. And, of course, you need athletes as well, and that's what your job is.

> **"At most schools 'diversity' is an important word when it comes to admissions."**

Like it or not, your job crosses lines with the admissions office. I did a study of all the students who were in the Naval Academy's admissions system and how we had picked them up. Forty-five percent of the African-American students in our admissions system had been identified by coaches. So unbeknownst to our admissions office personnel, who are under tremendous pressure to recruit African-American students, the school's coaching staff was doing most of their work. This is just one example of how the two departments work together.

Working Within NCAA Guidelines

We all take exams on NCAA rules. The NCAA manual is the most important tool you have. But just as important in the recruiting business is your school's college catalog. Whether you realize it or not, you really need to know what's contained in the catalog.

There are restrictions on what can and can't be sent to an athletic recruit. But don't let your efforts be short-changed by an uninformed admissions office. Familiarize yourself with the brochures and literature they're sending out. Remind admissions personnel that if something is being mailed out to all students who are applying to the school, there's no reason that athletes shouldn't receive it.

At the same time, take advantage of the equipment, manpower and technology your admissions office might have when it comes to the mailing process.

One day I was walking through a coach's office and there were a couple of graduate assistants hand-addressing dozens of envelopes. I asked them what was going on. "We're going to have a camp this summer so we're sending flyers out to all the high schools in Pennsylvania, Maryland, New Jersey, Delaware, Virginia and North Carolina," they said.

Because I had worked in the admissions office at one time, I knew that it had computer-generated labels for every high school in Pennsylvania, Maryland, New Jersey and Delaware. Not only that, but there was a machine that automatically folded the information and stuffed it into the envelope. So the lesson to be learned is, if you have a good working relationship with the people who run the mailroom and this type of equipment in the admissions office, you can save yourself a lot of time and hard work.

The Admissions System

Once a student-athlete you're recruiting is placed in the admissions office system, he or she will begin receiving volumes of mail from them. As an athletic office representative, you have limits on what you can send to them. But your school's admissions office doesn't have limits on what they can send out. And you'd be surprised at what some admissions systems send.

> **"You'd be surprised at what some admissions systems send out to your prospects."**

When my son was a junior in high school, I was absolutely amazed at the amount of materials he got from schools I had never heard of. I always thought the Air Force Academy had the world's biggest recruiting budget, but there were some schools that were sending out letters to him at least once a week.

And it makes a difference. My son said, "Dad, they really like me there," and I kept saying, "Glenn, if they only saw your SAT score, they don't know a thing about you." But they continued to inundate him with information on their school and their programs.

With your admissions office sending out so much information, it's important for you to know what the athletes you're recruiting are receiving. It can become very uncomfortable for you when you're talking to a recruit or their parents and they ask a question about something they've received and you don't know what it is.

Some of the material sent out to your recruits can inadvertently be discouraging to your recruit. A computer-generated letter might tell your recruit that his or her SAT scores are so low that there's not a chance of getting accepted. And if the recruit's name is in the system early in the process, it could be that their PSAT or junior-year SAT and ACT scores are triggering this response. Hopefully, the student's scores are going to rise with each test-taking effort. But the admissions office computer will say the initial view of the student is that his/her SAT score is not good enough to get in.

It can present a very embarrassing situation where you call up the recruit, telling them what a great opportunity they'll have to play at your school, and how you think their academics are good enough to get them in. Then, the next day, the recruit calls you and says, "Coach, I just got a letter from this guy in admissions and he says I can't get in your school." So you need to be very careful that there's not some happy little computer over there attacking all your hard work. That's why I say it's worthwhile knowing what's going on in the admissions office. You can help yourself out; they can help you out.

Serving the Student-Athlete

Some of today's students receive overwhelming pressure from parents to succeed. They want Jimmy or Sally to be a lawyer or a doctor. Inevitably, they'll ask you, "Can I be a lawyer?" You have to legitimately answer that question. Do they have the academic credentials to succeed in that field? Does your school have the program to get them to their goal? And does that particular program have an available spot for your recruit?

You have to know the answers to these questions. And you have to answer those questions as honestly as you can.

> **Evaluate your program against the student's needs. Does your school have the program they are seeking?**

Another important thing to know is what your admissions office is telling students who visit the campus or who call to ask questions. This means taking time to sit in on an admissions briefing. This will help you decide which recruits would benefit from this type of information.

I had the opportunity to experience this first-hand, when my son and I visited a school on the east coast.

The first words out of the mouth of the school's assistant director of admissions was, "If you aren't taking all advanced placement and honors courses, why are you sitting in this room?"

That may have been a legitimate question for most applicants, but I'm not so sure I'd want some of our athletic recruits to hear that the first time they hit the campus.

The Campus Tour

In addition to the academic briefing, another integral part of familiarizing a recruit with the school is the campus tour. If you're new to the school, this will help *you* get up to speed, as well. And even if you aren't new, this will help you know what's being said about the school.

At the Naval Academy, we have a lot of tours. We have our own athletic department tour and we train our tour guides. The admissions department also trains our tour guides, because they get a lot of academic questions like, "How does my son or daughter get into the Naval Academy?" We also have a lot of non-academic tour groups from Annapolis and we work with them to keep them up to speed on everything the Academy has to offer.

I've tagged along behind some of these tour groups and heard some tremendously erroneous information. Whether your school uses a tour service, or it's your athletic department personnel or the admissions office conducting a tour, it's important that the tour guides are properly trained. Make sure they know the correct answers to athletic department questions.

The Admissions Process

If you didn't have the luxury of having attended the school where you're coaching, it's important to familiarize yourself with the school and the programs it offers. And just as important in selling your school is knowing how the admissions office is "selling" itself. It can be embarrassing if the school's admissions office is telling a recruit one thing and you're telling them something else.

By working closely with your admissions coordinator, you'll know just how hard you can push the envelope on academics...and how much paperwork you'll need to get a recruit in the door.

At the Naval Academy, our admissions packets are pretty thick. This becomes a factor when we're competing against a lot of other schools for a recruit. Some athletes – especially football players – are notorious for not filling out the forms your admissions office requires. They don't take the time or they don't want to take the

time, or in some cases, they don't have the time.

Today's student-athletes – and high school students in general – have many more constraints on their time than students did 20 years ago. Fred Hargin, the dean of admissions at Princeton, has a saying that's worth passing on to the parents of the student-athletes that you're recruiting: "Admissions packets are not like fine wine. They do not get better with age."

Once you're convinced a student you're recruiting is genuinely interested in your school, pressure them to get that admissions packet completed and returned. This is especially important if you're at a school that has a rolling admission.

At the Academy, our first admissions board is in October. If your application is complete, the admissions board might not be able to tell you if you'll be admitted, but it can at least let you know what your chances of getting in are at that point. This helps you and the recruit – especially if you're trying to out-recruit somebody else.

> **"The essay or personal statement can help your prospect's chances of admission."**

It's also important to know what's in the admissions packet and to know what's required of a recruit to fill out. A recruit may very well call you with a question about it. And, at the same time, you can give them advice on what to do or what not to do.

A lot of schools require an essay or a personal statement as part of the application. On the athletic side, it's usually to the advantage of the applicant to have a coach write something. Something along the lines of "I've met this young woman… she's very involved… has a strong work ethic… good athlete… good family, etc." This means something to an admissions board.

So when you take the time to write your recommendation for a student-athlete, remember this is your chance to personalize that student for the admissions board. Otherwise he or she is just another name on a piece of paper.

Likewise, tell your potential recruit to take time to write a carefully worded statement. Give them tips on what the admissions board is looking for and impress upon them how important it is to read the directions. If your school requires something to be typed, make sure the applicant is using a word processor and is spell-checking it before it's printed out. If it can be hand-written, have them type it in a word processor, spell check it, print it and then copy it onto the application.

Special Programs

Your school's admissions office is often running several recruiting programs of its own. You can take advantage of their efforts by knowing what's available to a potential recruit and running them through the admissions program. While we're all trying to recruit the best athlete, there are some marginal athletes who won't make or break your program but they will be expected to contribute. Your budget might not allow you to work on them as strongly, but there may be an admissions program which can help you lure them to your program.

One program often made available to all potential students is an "overnight visit." It doesn't count as an official visit and, although the athlete may have to pay $10 or $20 to stay in the dormitory and eat there, it's a great way to get that kid on campus for a weekend.

This type of visit is also a good situation for an athlete who's recruiting you and won't go away. Or even for the mom or dad who have an athlete who's recruiting you and just won't go away.

Summer Programs

A lot of schools have various summer programs, and as you identify juniors who might be strongly recruited, this may be a good way to get them interested in your school.

Getting them on campus in the summer makes your job easier in the fall when you're talking to them in the recruiting process. They've been on campus and are famil-

> **"Get prospects on campus early – use your summer programs to get them interested."**

iar with your school. Obviously, you're not going to get all your blue-chip recruits to do this, but this is a great opportunity for your secondary recruits.

It's also a way to help them feel a little special, and something they can tell their friends and family about. It's also going to pay off when you talk to them later since they'll know what you're talking about when you refer to something on campus or a teacher they may have met.

The Admissions Office

I've tried to stress the importance of knowing what people in the admissions office are saying. Your admissions coordinator can tell you who on the admissions office staff can help you out. People in the admissions office are just as concerned about the diversity of the school and the athletic success of the school as they are in the academic side and the make-up of the class size.

Every school needs a certain percentage of women and minorities, athletes and academicians. The admissions office is in the same business as you and they're sympathetic to your requirements, so they're often willing to help.

When you set up weekend visits for recruits – both official and unofficial – think about the admissions people. They're there to help.

Another way your admissions office can lend a hand in recruiting is a student "call system." The program has current students call potential students at night or on weekends to entice them to come to their school. Normally, the call system targets the blue-chip academic types, minorities and sometimes even students they'd like to get in the school band.

But there's no reason why they can't call your athletic recruits as well. Just be careful that no rules are broken in the process. Again, it's important to communicate and work closely with the admissions department to ensure that this doesn't happen.

The Faculty Representative

At schools where I've coached, each team had a faculty representative and each type was a military representative, meaning one of the military officers stationed at the Academy.

Our lacrosse coach had a great program on Saturday mornings for unofficial and official visits. He would conduct a mini seminar which would include a session with the faculty representative. He would talk to the recruits and tell them what they could accomplish at the school. He knew, too, because the faculty representative would travel with the team. He was also sympathetic to our recruiting challenges. So it's nice having a faculty representative and it's helpful to have them around on weekends when recruits are visiting.

It's also worthwhile having somebody from the admissions office there as well. This representative should have a good understanding of your program and what you're trying to accomplish with your student-athletes. It gives the student another perspective, separate from the athletic side.

Interacting With Other School Groups

> **"People outside the athletic department often see things differently."**

The schools I've been associated with have what's called "liaison officers," who interview all candidates for admission. It's a requirement, in fact. We have about 2,000 liaison officers across the country who interview students who are applying to the Naval Academy or the other service academies. I know MIT has a similar system, so be aware of this program if your school has one in place.

Whenever someone outside your school's athletic department talks to one of your recruits, you should know what their approach will be. Not everyone played sports and some people didn't struggle in the classroom like some athletes do. It's been my experience that sometimes someone from one of these groups will interview one of your athletes and you'll never get them back.

That's why your athletic department needs to make a conscious decision on whether it really wants the alumni group or a liaison officer interviewing your prospective student-athlete. They see life a little differently than we see life in the athletic recruiting business.

A Good Work Ethic

The old saying has always been "work harder." It's said most often when recruiting is not going well, or when a team's win-loss record is not what it should be. Well, if I've heard it one time, I've heard it a million times from coaches who have programs that are struggling.

But rather than work harder, you should work smarter. Learn to take advantage of today's technology. Twenty years ago there weren't any fax machines. There weren't any computers. There wasn't overnight mail or even e-mail. Now we're inundated with fast, easy communication methods. Technology can make things easy on you when you need something right away, like an application. But know the limits your school places on such correspondence. Some admissions boards do not accept faxed responses of any kind. Again, that's why it's helpful to have a friend in the admissions office who can make exceptions now and then when you really need something fast.

Passing Over A Recruit

Along with a smarter work ethic is being a good person as well. There are a lot of students you pass over in the recruiting process. Maybe they sent you an application or filled out one of your questionnaires. But, for one reason or another, they don't fill your needs. I think you owe it to that young man or young woman to pass their application on to admissions. It gives everyone a fair chance and can prevent a situation like the one I'm about to describe.

> **"You owe it to *all* your prospects to pass their applications on to admissions."**

I picked up the phone one day just before the start of classes and the woman on the other line asked me when the bus was coming by to pick up her son. I put her on hold, rushed over to my computer and looked up his name. He wasn't in my computer. In fact, I hadn't ever heard of him.

His mother said, "Your coach came by our house and sat in our living room and told us that Bobby could go to your school."

I asked, "Did you ever get an admissions packet from us?" She said, "No."

"Did the coach ever call you back?" I asked. She replied, "No, he told me he could go to your school."

So here's a kid in New Jersey waiting for the blue and gold bus to stop by his house. His bags are packed and he's out on the front porch. It was really sad and it wasn't fair.

Had the coach forwarded the student's packet over to admissions early on, that infamous computer would have sent him a letter telling him to get his scores up or he wouldn't be accepted.

Unfortunately, at my school, these types of situations aren't reviewed by the president of the university, they go to a member of Congress. So in this case, it wasn't good. This worst-case scenario should stress the importance of advancing students you are no longer interested in on to the admissions office.

Summary

You are the artist. You are the person who can get the student-athlete you want, one you think can help your program. He or she may not quite measure up to what the admissions committee wants, but you can bring that person to life. And that's your job. You can bring that person to the doorstep and then help them get through the admissions board.

> **"You are the person who can get the student-athlete you want."**

There are all kinds of people in this world. If you didn't know this already, you should. You don't know who they are, or where they're from, but they want to come to your school and play sports.

Unfortunately, great athletes are few and far between. Your admissions office should have people who have the ability to help you find athletes who aren't the blue-chippers but who can still help your program out.

It can be as simple as having admissions include a piece of paper in a packet which says, "I'd like to try out for this sport, and here's why," or "Here's my height, my weight, my speed."

Every once in a while you'll stumble across a future blue-chipper in this manner. All because you got a second chance in the recruiting process through your effort and cooperation with your school's admissions office.

Author Profile: Dave Davis

Dave Davis has over 15 years of college admissions experience. After completing a successful 25-year career in the United States Navy, the last three years as admissions director at the U.S. Naval Academy, he joined the Navy Athletic Association staff as a recruiting and admissions specialist. He is currently serving as executive assistant to the athletic director at the U.S. Naval Academy, specializing in admissions and academic support.

TRADE SECRETS FOR RECRUITING TO THE SMALL SCHOOL

A Panel with Mike Evans, Dick Foster and Mary Yori

Q: *What advantages do you sell to recruits on your specific competitive level?*

Mike Evans: At the Division I level, I felt we really never had a chance to analyze prospects and really get close to them like I have at the NAIA level. In Division I, we had a lot of regulations that kept us from really getting to know our players and developing them the way they should be developed. I've found that the more time we spent with players, the bigger impact we could have on them. But the rules in NCAA Division I kept pulling us away from them. We felt like the more time we could spend around them, regulating their study halls and time, the better. In NAIA, we can check on them a lot better than we could in Division I, where I didn't know for sure if they'd gone to class or not. Now I have a daily report. Parents like the idea that I get a daily report from all the teachers. If a player misses a class, they know they have a standard five mile run if they do.

I think the regulations are so stringent on the Division I level that they sometimes keep players from being able to develop. Especially in baseball, where we feel like practice games and things we do in the fall really help us get ready for the spring. It also helps develop the personality of our team, so we can work together as a team. So having more games and having more practice time helps us get to know players a lot better.

Players know that we have to earn all the money that we need. I think in Division I, a lot of stuff is given to the players. In contrast, our players have to *earn* their spring trip, *earn* the places they go. They know it's all going to be taken away from them if they don't maintain a good grade point average and do the things that they need to do. Our players know they don't have a spring trip next year if they don't keep their grade point averages where they belong.

Mary Yori: One advantage is that Division II is competitive, but sometimes there is not quite the business end of things that I think some student-athletes feel at the Division I level. Sometimes Division I can feel like it's not fun anymore; that it's all work and no fun. It's all business. It's all big-time Division I sports. I think we have an advantage in Division II in that we do have more fun. It's still very, very competitive. You can still be very successful at the level we're playing at, but winning is not the only thing that we are interested in at the Division II level.

The philosophy is much different at Division II than it is at Division I. We are interested in shaping a well-rounded individual who has good grades. We want to make sure that they get a degree, and that they're involved in the community. We try to stress that in our recruiting. I think it's important because we're going to be able to put better leaders and better people in our communities if we can stress *those* kinds of things as opposed to just winning and losing. The key is stressing the intangibles to convince them that they want to be a well-rounded person.

Dick Foster: There's one simple thing that I love about junior college that I don't think you can have anyplace else. You only have to worry about yourself, because you're doing it all. You are doing the coaching, you are doing the recruiting, and you are doing the academics. You're doing everything it takes to make that program work.

> **"It's very difficult to work under somebody who didn't hire you in the beginning."**

Anytime you're on a big staff, there are intangibles that serve to create a noose around your neck. You know that if this guy doesn't do his job and this other guy doesn't do his job either, that it's not going to happen. That's why when I went to the University of Oklahoma, I did not want to be tied to a football coach. It's difficult to work under somebody who didn't hire you in the very beginning.

Along this same line, you have to make up your mind – you have to really want to coach on a Division III level or you're going to be a failure. At one time, I thought I wanted to go back to a Division I school and coach. But then I remembered all the problems – like set recruiting times and having to literally recruit 365 days out of the year. That's probably what guided me to junior college.

Plus, in junior college, you have a better chance of controlling your destiny. It doesn't matter what level you're at, the fewer people you have to go through to get your job done, the higher the probability you are going to be successful.

If You're In Demand, Make Some Demands

When I went to Coffeyville, they wanted me. I found out later that I was the seventh coach in 10 years that the president had hired. The board of trustees told him, "You've been president here long enough. If you can't find a football coach who can come in and win and be successful, then we're going to find a president with the ability to do that." I didn't know that when I was hired, but he sought me out for the job.

I made some demands. I said, "I don't want to work through other people. I don't want to have to go through an athletic director, department head, and 19 different people to get a decision made." He simply told me, "Fine, that's what will happen." I had to remind the president several times during our working relationship, "You have promised me this," and we got it through. As a coach, you have to make two lists: one list of positives about your program and what you have to sell, and second, a list of negatives. You certainly don't want to recruit using the negatives; you want to use the positives.

When I was at Fort Scott Junior College, I had nothing to sell except one thing – me. I had no record at that time except my background in high school. People didn't want to know about my record in high school; I was smart enough to know that. Once I got to Coffeyville, we had some positive things and I started a list of positives.

Q: *How do you organize your recruiting program on your level to attract a top quality student-athlete year after year?*

Mary Yori: There is some method to the madness, believe it or not. Sometimes it feels like it's helter skelter when you're recruiting because it's such a big area and recruiting is obviously very important. I think the biggest part of the process is the networking. Meet with other coaches in your community, in areas that you choose to recruit from.

> **"Sometimes it feels like it's helter skelter when you're recruiting, but there is method to the madness."**

For instance, the University of Nebraska at Omaha is kind of an urban campus in the city, and we generally recruit out of the state, in surrounding states. We don't go much further than that. That's not to say we won't go to a tournament now and then and watch good talent. But everyone is limited to their budget.

The main thing, whether you're recruiting in the Midwest or you're recruiting across the country, you have to network with coaches to find the best players in the country. You can do that very simply. It's no secret – everybody pretty much knows who the best players are, but you have to find out who those players are by finding things like All-State teams and All-City teams. Get in touch with people who run the state tournaments for the high schools, whether that is a state activities group or whether that is a high school association. But you need to make a list of who you are going to go after. That's the number one thing. Then you go from there.

Finding Athletes That Fit Your Philosophy

Who wants to come to your school? You have athletes who say right up front, I only want Division I, period. Fine, don't even spend time with them, because you're wasting your time. Move on to where you can find the right people to fit into the philosophy that you have for your level.

In recruiting, there are lots of details. Have a plan for what you want to do. Try to find out if the athlete has the same philosophy and the same personality you have. I think it's important to coach players with similar personalities to yours, because I think, in the end, you're going to be much more successful. If you are a mild-mannered, laid-back, easy-going coach, it's going to be tough to coach a bunch of hotheaded, out-of-control players. So I think you need to find players who fit your philosophy.

You want upbeat, positive players who want to go out and practice and play as hard as they can. I look for certain characteristics in players. You have to make a decision – what's right for you? Do you want 15 players on your team who are the most hard-nosed, competitive, "get out there and practice everyday, go at each other's throat and they hate each other on the floor, but they win" players? If that's what you want, then terrific. You need to find players who fit into your philosophy.

Dick Foster: When I first started, I had two instruments: me and the telephone. I didn't know anything about letters or other recruiting tools at that particular time. Once I got established, I learned a lot.

> **"In coaching junior college, you have very few rules."**

Everything goes back to your positives and negatives, your list of the things that you want to sell. And, needless to say, your budget and how much money you actually have to spend.

There were five instruments that I used to help us in the recruiting process. The first is the telephone. That's one of the great things about coaching in junior college – you have very few rules. You don't have to worry about too many restrictions.

Second was a newsletter. It was a way to communicate with booster club members as well as prospects. Your budget will determine whether you can afford to send a newsletter out once a month, every three months, every six months, or once a year.

Third, I was inspired by our school newspaper. I thought, "Boy, that thing is cheap to make," and so we made a recruiting newspaper. I went to the woman who was in charge of our school newspaper for help. I followed the format of a college newspaper, but I put in all the things that I thought were important in recruiting.

Next, I spent a bunch of my time (because I didn't have any money in my budget) on a pre-game press guide. I went out and sold ads to a couple of business people, and I made a simple pre-game press guide that I did everything with. Later, I figured out it was an assistant's job to go out and sell advertisements to make a fancy program that was sold at the ballgames, but also was a great recruiting tool.

Finally, use television as a tool if you can. We were very fortunate, because after about the fifth year I was at Coffeyville, we got a TV station and I had my own TV show. We put together an 8-10 minute segment on highlights from a football standpoint and then an 8-minute segment on academics. After you get finished with the original cost of producing it, you're talking about $2-$3 and maybe $1 to send it out. You can ask for the tape back, but you know you're never going to get it back.

The Future of Recruiting

I think 5-10 years from now, recruiting is going to be more curtailed than what it is now, as far as rules and regulations. In the future, a lot of recruiting for some sports may have to come directly out of the admissions and recruitment offices on campus. We already worked closely with these departments. I met once a month with all the people on our campus who were involved, in some way, with student recruiting.

When I got to Oklahoma, I could not believe what poor quality literature we were sending out to student prospects. They finally upgraded the quality of literature that was available, which helped me, because anything they could send out, we could send out. They spent $30,000 to create a tape that they sent to prospective students. There was nothing on the tape about athletics. But I could give the admissions department a list of our top 50 football prospects and they could send that out to them. It's a great recruiting tool and it's selling the University of Oklahoma.

Mike Evans: As a recruiter at the University of Nebraska, I went all over the nation recruiting Division I players. To compete in the NAIA, I have to get the same type of players that I was getting at the Division I level. It's pretty tough to do that.

The first thing I tried to do was establish areas where I had really close-knit ties. These were places where I knew the coaches in that area and they liked me as a friend, not just as a coach. One of the first things I thought of was that the school is a block away from the Mormon Church.

I have a very good friend in Utah who's a Mormon, and I knew Brigham Young University didn't recruit a lot of the local players. They go national in recruiting and they don't always go after some of the better local players. Just by going in and talking to these people, I've been able to recruit some of the best players in Utah. We have a Mormon church close to school and I don't require my players to play on Sunday. If we have a game on Sunday, I certainly honor their religious views.

The parents like it. I'm able to go out to Utah and have dinner with everyone and I'm able to show our highlight tapes. I'm able to go out and sell parents on our program at Bellevue University.

I don't even have to see these players, because I trust the people out there. I know these people would not send me a player who doesn't fit into my viewpoint of how the game should be played. I don't believe in cussing. I don't do it.

I want my players to be able to sit in the dugout without other players throwing bats or helmets or using foul language.

So to attract good players, I have to trust my friends. I have to ask, "Who's the best player in your area? Do they fit my philosophy?" Then I have to trust my contacts, that they can play. I cannot go see everybody play. If you get burned once, you'll know better the next time.

The Numbers Game

In small schools, for the most part, numbers are very important. When I got hired at Bellevue University, they said, "Numbers is money." How many people you brought into the program was the key. I said, "Okay, I'll bring in 50 athletes, but I want to have a scholarship fund, so much per athlete that I get into the program." I may not use that much money for every athlete – some athletes I may get in for free – but I wanted to have a carryover value.

> **"It's a money game and you just have to go out there and do it."**

With some schools, you can't use those bargaining tools, but that's what I did. So the more people I could bring in that school, the more leverage I had. Our school's not very expensive; it costs approximately $3,000 per year. I showed the school that even if I gave a $500 scholarship to everybody, they were still going to make $2,500 on every student-athlete. It's a money game and you just have to go out there and do it.

Using Technology

I think video highlights are a great idea. We film every game during the year and most of our practices. We believe it's a good teaching tool. We have a highlight tape of all the home runs and the pitcher striking players out and we're able to send tapes to parents. If their child pitches a good ballgame, but they're in California, we can pick out highlights and send it to the parents. The parents can see that home run they hit or that good ballgame they had. The worst thing in the world is a parent not being able to see their child play. To be able to at least save their big moments for parents is something that really works in the recruiting area. I bring tapes along, and I tell parents we can do the same thing for them.

Recruit Locally

I also think you need to recruit locally. But you have to watch so that you don't get burned. A local player can really hurt you in your recruiting if he can't play and he ends up sitting on the bench. I'm much better off having a player from California come in who can't play than a player from Nebraska who can't play. I recruit that Omaha player, but I tell them they may not be able to play. I also tell his parents that he may not be able to play. I go after the best players in the state.

Some of them, I know I'm not going to get. But I go to their house and I talk to them and I give them the first offer, before there's even other people coming to see them. When they sign somewhere else, I write them a nice letter congratulating them about going to that school. And I add a note on there, "If anything should ever happen, you know Bellevue University will always want you."

In my first six years at Bellevue, I got at least one transfer that didn't work out at a Division I school each year.

Q. *Do you recruit players you know you cannot get? Why or why not?*

Mike Evans: I do go after players I can't get, and the reason why is because of transfers back in. At my level, I have to get the best junior college players around. I have to reload because every year I'll lose four or five juniors to the draft, if I'm recruiting the right players.

> "Recruit players you can't get, even if it's just to show your interest."

If I'm not recruiting the right players, it doesn't matter. The way the professional draft works right now, players know that if you don't hold them back, that they'll want to sign. That philosophy probably doesn't work with some other sports, but we don't hold anybody back in our school.

If the player is able to sign we say, "Good-bye. Thanks. Get your education paid for and come back and finish up at our school someday." We don't have any full scholarships. So if they get their education paid for, they have received more than I could give them.

I think you have to recruit players that you can't get. Just show them your interest, especially if they're local. With out-of-state prospects, it doesn't usually make a difference. But sometimes, you'll get out-of-state prospects who remembered that you were the first to contact them and if it doesn't work out, they will call. Going after prospects you know you won't get can be discouraging, but it doesn't have to be. Turn it around to be a positive.

Mary Yori: I don't think you can really say there's a player out there that you cannot get. My philosophy is, "Sure, there's going to be players that turn me down, but I'm not afraid to go after any player that I feel is a worthy player and has the credentials to play. I go talk to them, send the letters and make the telephone calls. I do whatever is appropriate at the time.

You contact the best players. Maybe they don't want to go to a Division I school – for whatever reason. Maybe it's the coaching or their personalities don't match. So don't be afraid. And don't back down.

Q. *With a very limited budget, what are your top priorities in recruiting?*

Dick Foster: When I was at Fort Scott, we had a very limited budget, but telephone and mail use was not charged to my budget. When I went to Coffeyville, I was smart enough to ask that telephone and mail use be excluded from my budget. They agreed to keep those two items out of my budget, which was critical, because telephone and mail use are the two most important things in recruiting.

> **"Get the maximum you can out of the admissions office."**

You also have to work to get the maximum out of the admissions office that you can. I finally convinced our president that it would help everyone if they helped us, because they were going out and trying to recruit students like we were. My president wanted to increase enrollment and he saw the value in us working together. I think working with the admissions people is very important when you have a limited budget.

Mike Evans: You have a lot better chance of getting the budget you need if you can promise them something. Promise you will improve something in their program. Say, "I'm going to prove this and if I don't, then you can take it (the money) away from me. But I can guarantee you that I'm going to improve this area." It can be that you will bring in more students. We are going to win more. Our grade point average is going to be higher. We are going to graduate more students. You have to work those things into your budget.

When I first started at Bellevue, we had a ridiculously small budget. I know why the coaches that were there couldn't win – they didn't have the money. Our budget is 10 times bigger than it was when I first got there. Nobody is going to increase your budget by 10 times unless you prove to them that they're going to make money on what you're going to do. So you have to show them how your program, in the long run, is going to make money.

Mary Yori: You have to start with your local talent. Obviously, the more inexpensive player is going to be the local player. As you get outside the city and outside the state, it's going to cost you more money to bring in players.

I think another thing that is important as far as the budget goes is if you have a walk-on program. We try to convince prospects they can still be on a good team, even though they are not going to get any financial help from the athletic department. Also, look for players who will qualify for government money. Or, if they don't qualify, try your best to find resources on your campus. For example, if the student is an education major, there might be some kind of education scholarship available. If you know what is available on your campus, you can help students qualify for the help that is out there.

No matter what school you are at, you're never going to have the kind of budget that you would like to have, so you have to make do and you have to be a good salesman. We have to convince prospects that they should choose us because they love the game, not because financially they are going to get rich off of it.

Q. *What elements make up a campus visit for a recruit that comes to your school, and why do you schedule campus visits the way that you do?*

Mary Yori: A campus visit is obviously very important. An athlete needs to get to your campus to see what you have to offer and what you are all about. They can't just read about it in a flyer. They can't just be told about it on the telephone. I really think it's important that they get to the campus and visit. There are actually people who commit to colleges and sign letters of intent without visiting campuses. It does happen. I think they're in for a world of shock. They are expecting what they see – this beautiful picture in some kind of a viewbook and then it's a totally different scenario once they get there.

> **"Players who commit without a campus visit are in for a world of shock."**

What to Include on the Campus Visit – If In Doubt, Just Ask

In terms of what to include on a campus visit, it depends on the individual. We have conducted exit interviews with some of our athletes, asking them what they liked and disliked about the campus visit. What would they like to see be done better? The answers were, as you might expect, totally across the board. Some players didn't like meeting with an advisor, other players said they liked the part where they met with an advisor. So you're going to get all kinds of different answers.

The best scenario might be to ask the athlete. When you're talking to him or her on the phone, ask, "What would you like to see happen on this campus visit? What would you be interested in doing or having done on the campus visit? We have options. You can meet with an advisor from your department. You can meet with the athletes. You can stay with the athletes. You can stay in a motel. We have a lot of different choices." Getting their input is important.

One of the most important things about a campus visit is for the players to spend time with you as a coach and also spend time with the other players on the team. They need to spend time in the dorms or the apartments with them and eat lunch or dinner with them. We want them to ask true questions of what's going on in our program. "What it's all about? Do you really like it here? Do you like the coach? How is practice run?" I encourage the athletes that come to campus to ask questions because they're not always going to ask you, but they will ask the other student-athletes.

Dick Foster: In the 14 years I was at Coffeyville, I never brought one out-of-state recruit in for a visit because we didn't have the money to bring them in. I went to their homes instead. A lot of times, out-of-state players who did choose us were in deep shock when they finally got to Coffeyville, Kansas.

Because of the things that I wanted to accomplish on the campus visit, we would bring in large numbers of in-state recruits. We might bring in 35 prospects on a weekend because I tried to do it on three weekends. I did it that way because it was cheaper for me to do it that way and they needed to know that when they got there in the fall, there were going to be 100 people out on the practice field and only half of those guys were going to end up playing. The other half were either going to redshirt or they were going to leave and go to other programs. The second thing was that I worked really hard to get the faculty involved on the student visit. I thought that was important, because other junior colleges weren't doing this. I didn't want to tie down the faculty members to more than three weekends.

Categorize Your Recruits

Basically, I had two types of recruits. The first were those that I wanted to bring in to stay all night, and when we did this, we would try to plan it around a basketball game. I didn't want them in before Saturday afternoon. I wanted them there less than 20 hours on campus, because the longer you had them there, the more time they had to be unhappy with the visit.

> **"Use your faculty and your financial aid personnel to help you recruit student-athletes."**

I wanted every minute to be planned for them. That didn't mean that they were with the coaches all the time. On Sunday morning, the faculty came in and helped us. I would have as many faculty people there as I could muster and we had breakfast together. The faculty would sit and visit with the prospects according to their academic interest. We also had representatives from the financial aid department there. While they were meeting with the faculty and the financial aid people, I did my personal interviews over in the cafeteria in a room by itself. I wanted them out of there by noon on Sunday.

The second group of prospects were lower priority, so we would try to get them in some afternoon during the week.

Mike Evans: At Bellevue, we are not allowed to fly anybody in or pay for anybody's visit. They have to come and pay for their own visit, which really makes it tough. A lot of players come to our school without seeing the campus, which may be good, because there isn't much to see. We have made improvements on it, but a lot of high schools have better facilities than we have. We are not a very impressive campus to look at.

What I have to do is make sure our visits are great when they do come, because they sometimes take one look at our place and they're ready to walk out. I have a faculty member that just loves baseball come and talk to our recruits. I have our players come in. I let them talk all about our program. Then I'll talk to the recruits about what we do in our program. Then I'll say, "Okay, just ask our players. I'll get out of here and you can ask them any question you'd like." They ask them any question they want about our program and what we do. I think our players really sell our program.

Use Parents When Possible

The other thing is I have local parents come in. Parents like to hear stuff from other parents. They ask, "What was it like? Did he do everything that he said he was going to do? Did he take care of your child's education?"

For every out-of-state recruit that I have, I have one of my out-of-state parents call that parent and tell them what it was like being in our program. Coming into our place on visit, we show them a video about our program and highlights of everything that we do in the program. We have a visit with the players. We have a visit with a faculty member and we have a visit with the parents.

That's about it. If they stay overnight, we are allowed to let them stay in the apartments of our players – that's where I would like to have them stay anyway. We like to make them short and be concise about what we're going to do, who they are going to meet and have the people who love the program selling the program.

Q. *In summary, what are some of your trade secrets for recruiting to the small school?*

Mike Evans: You have to talk to the parents and emphasize what you have to offer – what type of atmosphere you have, what kind of grade point averages your players have, your study hall, tutoring and your job placement process after they graduate.

> "Emphasize what you have to offer to the recruit."

Second, build up a community base. This might not seem like it's part of recruiting, but I think it is. You have to get very involved with the community as far as doing things in the community. That may be running free clinics for kids.

I run clinics for children ages 7 all the way up to high school. We invite the parents to come along. We show them, step-by-step, what they can do to help their child develop. That shows the parents that you want to do something for the community and get involved. It shows that you care for your students – whether or not they are a great baseball player. If you show that you care, I think you're going to be successful in your recruiting.

Mary Yori: For starters, you have to answer the question, "Why would an athlete want to come to my school?" What are the positives? Then look at the negatives. Why would she not want to come to my school? Then you have to make a plan from there.

Second, go after athletes you want. Don't be afraid or back down. Go after the player that you think is the best player that will help make your program, or continue to make it, successful. Then you go through the steps – phone calls, correspondence, meeting with parents, getting them to campus (if possible), home visits, and whatever else it takes.

> **"The main thing is you have to be confident you have something to offer your prospects."**

But the main thing is you have to be able to feel very positive about your school. I think that's a key. You have to feel good about your department, feel good about your school and what you have to offer. If you can't feel good about that or you don't have a lot of positive things to say, then I would say that you might be in the wrong place. You have to be able to feel good and feel confident that you have a lot to offer prospects.

Dick Foster: The most important thing is you have a game plan. And your game plan needs to be written down. I think it's the responsibility of the head coach to be sure that you have an accurate game plan to have a successful recruiting program.

It bothers me when coaches spend hours and hours on Xs and Os and studying film and other people's coaching techniques, but don't spend time learning effective recruiting techniques. If you don't have a game plan, start writing one now. If you're an assistant coach and your head coach doesn't have one, then make one up and try to get him or her to go along with it. I think it is the responsibility of the head coach to have a checklist to be sure that the game plan is being executed.

We spend a lot of time preparing ourselves and our team to be successful on Saturday night. I have a checklist to make sure we do all those things. On Sunday morning, as I'm looking at film, I'm asking myself, "Did we fulfill this? Did we do this? Did we do that?" I use my checklist. I think the same thing is true as far as recruiting. You have to have a game plan.

The Importance of the Home and Campus Visits

The most critical thing in the recruiting process is the home visit of the head coach. If I could leave a message that would inspire you, the most important thing is the head coach's involvement in the home visit. If you're going to be a great coach and a great recruiter, you had better learn the techniques for a successful home visit, because it's critical. Barry Switzer was a master at being able to go into a home. It didn't make any difference if that prospect was from the ghettos or if he lived in a million dollar home – he knew how to adjust to that family situation. I think that is important and you had better get your skills developed in that area.

The last thing is the campus visit. I think you lose some and you gain some on every campus visit. You had better spend a lot of time working hard on your game plan and seeing that it is executed properly.

If you're weak as a head coach on the home visit or if you're weak as far as your on-campus visits, you had better work on developing those skills if you are going to be successful recruiting athletes to your small school.

Panel Profiles:

Mike Evans is the head baseball coach and assistant athletic director at Bellevue (NE) University. A former University of Nebraska-Lincoln assistant coach, he is a National NAIA Coach-of-the-Year award winner. Mike has 15 years of college recruiting experience and his 1995 Bruins team won the NAIA World Series national championship.

Dick Foster was director of recruiting for all sports for the University of Oklahoma athletic department for eight years. With over 30 years of college recruiting experience, his coaching stops include Fort Scott (KS) Community College, Coffeyville (KS) Community College and the University of Kansas. Dick is currently serving as a volunteer coach with his son, head football coach Skip Foster at Coffeyville (KS) Community College.

Mary Yori is head softball coach at the University of Nebraska at Omaha. She is a two-time National NCAA Division II Coach-of-the-Year award winner and a seven-time regional Coach-of-the-Year award winner. The former Creighton University All-American has 10 years of college recruiting experience and has taken her Mavericks teams to four consecutive Division II National Finals appearances.

How to Write a More Effective Recruiting Letter

by Ernie Nestor

Both positive and negative recruiting is done by mail. Usually, we think of mail as a helpful tool in recruiting. But the mail could also be used in a negative sense, so the two sort of go hand in hand. You find yourself in situations where negative recruiting can be done quite easily through the mail; it can be done just by scanning newspaper articles. There was a time when schools in our conference used to get each other's school newspapers in order to know what was going on.

I coached at the University of California-Berkeley. If you're familiar with Cal-Berkeley, it isn't hard to find something going on at that school to put in the paper. I was there for just three years and in that time, there were some unbelievable things going on. An article even appeared in *People* magazine about a student going to class without any clothes on. It's just an unusual atmosphere and there's no way to explain it.

"Politically fertile ground," is, I guess, what they call it. Everybody has views and some of them are very, very unique. Some of them are unbelievable. The anti-apartheid movement was incredibly strong at Cal. Some very positive work came out of that. But it also seemed to always occur in November and April, usually right around signing day. It would come up in recruiting. Our prospects would receive articles in the mail, saying what had happened on the campus the other day. We'd say, "Well, that's very true; it did happen."

Cal is one of those schools that will never lose the image that people have of it from the 1960s. We just used to address it by saying, "Hey, you know these are real issues in our society. These people are really interested in these issues."

Because of the power of words, be careful what you write. What you put into print, make sure you're willing to read about on the front page of the *Washington Post*, because that's where it might end up. The other thing you have to remember is that the things you write last forever. When you put them in writing, they last forever. You might see them show up on the front page of the local paper's sports section a year later or even longer.

People are fairly cynical. They don't know what to believe about how things are in college athletics. We could use some good public relations, because most of the news about recruiting focuses on violations and sanctions.

Play By the Rules

Obviously, because of changes in the NCAA rules, the whole situation has changed. They have limited phone calls, and limited contact. Everything has been limited, including mail. Previously, the NCAA had rules that said what you couldn't do. You could fill in around that, as opposed to what you can and can't do now. Now they have specifically said – for the first time – you can only do *these* things. One of the things you cannot do anymore is reproduce newspaper articles. It used to be, if we had a great win, we would cut out the newspaper article, photocopy it and send it out. You can't do that anymore.

The first thing – and most important thing – is to know and understand the rules that you are operating under. They are much more specific now than they've ever been before. The rules will have a lot to do with what you can actually send out.

New Opportunities

But it also opened up a new area of opportunity. Before, the athletic department had been very specific in sending out their own things. Now, you really have to get around your campus and find out what is also available to send out.

> **"If you coach at a competitive institution, watch how admissions people recruit."**

The basic rule regarding what you can send to a prospective student-athlete is, "whatever is available for all prospective students who may want to come to the institution."

The first thing you should do is go right over to admissions, the financial aid department and anyplace else where you can line up information that can be used in your recruiting. Some of these departments are putting out some nice things.

If you're at an institution that needs to have students, that is in a competitive situation for students, watch the admissions people go to work. Admissions people who are trying to recruit kids who have high SATs will cut each other's hearts out. They have no mercy, these people.

I don't mean they're unethical. I mean they are just as aggressive as can be. Money is no object. They give students everything they want. When they get involved in recruiting one of these top academic students, they offer them a full ride, and then start looking for what kind of job they can get them in the summer. It is very, very competitive.

When you are looking at students who have scored 1400, 1500 or 1600 on the SAT, these are highly sought-after students. There is tremendous recruiting going on in the academic sector that many people are not aware of. They are aggressive in trying to attract these top-level students to their institution.

These are the things that you need to find out about. We take every prospect we have on campus to talk with an admissions officer. During that process, we always look around to see what the admissions department has. We always pick up a few things, things we may not have already sent. If you go over to admissions, you will find a lot more material than you ever thought was available.

Develop a Schedule

We developed a calendar form to track our mailings. Across the top are dates and down the side are the names. It's set up in a column format. To start out, we have certain mailings that go out on a particular date. We have a schedule to our mailings. As these mailings go out, we just check off on our form the prospects that receive them. If we decide we want to get involved with a prospect mid-stream, we add his name to the list, look across and check the status of our mailing effort and then we bring him up to speed with the back mailings.

Photocopy machines make it a lot easier. All you have to do is keep one of everything. Then you just go back and photocopy them and send them out to bring him up to speed with where you are. It's vital to keep records.

> **"If we decide we want to recruit a new prospect, we just add his name to the form."**

So if you find out about a new prospect, Johnny Jones, on the first of August, and you have been sending out mailings since the first of June, then you have a two-month period, maybe five or six mailings, you want to catch Johnny up on. You can do that with periodic mailings.

Sometimes if we get a prospect really late in the year, we want to get that information to him as soon as possible, so we may send him a lot of things at once to catch him up to speed.

The Power of Literature

I have two daughters. When it came time for them to pick a college to attend, they chose their colleges from recruiting literature sent out from the admissions departments at the schools. That was amazing to me.

My two daughters have had the benefit of growing up on college campuses around the country. They had been to every campus in the ACC when they were very young kids. And yet, they picked their colleges from literature.

They said to me, "Wow! This is the school." I said, "Why do you want to go there?" They answered, "Because I've looked over their information. I've read their information. It really seems like a neat place to go to school."

I was stunned. I didn't think anybody ever picked a school like that. I didn't think anybody even looked at that stuff. We send it out because everybody sends it out. Why would anybody look at it? Everybody's sending it.

I have to admit, my daughters picked good schools. They read over the materials, they knew about the student body, they looked at the campus – all from literature and pictures. Of course, we made campus visits, but the importance of that literature taught me a lot.

Obviously, this won't always work. But don't overlook the power of literature. That's why we set up scheduled mailings. When you get into the process, I think it is very important that you mail literature, not only to the prospect and his parents, but also to the high school coach.

Work with the Guidance Counselors

I think specific mailings have to be aimed at the guidance counselor. In today's college athletics, the academic rules are changing rapidly. The mis-information out there is probably as great as the information available.

Of course, there are problems inherent with guidance counselors; there's one for every 500 students. It's amazing. You call a guidance department and there may be three people working in there, and the school may have 1800 students. So you know the students are really not going to get a lot of one-on-one guidance. So you need to get the guidance people up to speed. Consider making a personal phone call to the guidance counselor.

> **"The guidance counselor is very important in getting information to prospects."**

We've had some success with calling guidance counselors. We ask the prospect, "Who is your senior counselor?" Then we call and say, "We're recruiting Johnny Jones and we'd like to send you some information that's really vital to Johnny." She says, "Well, we've really never dealt with this before." So we explain that Johnny is a young man with an opportunity to get a basketball scholarship at a pretty good school. But, we tell them, it's very important that certain things be done with some speed at various times in the process.

Guidance counselors are great people, but they're just tremendously overworked, and getting through to them and getting them interested is very important.

If you promise to send them information, you must follow up. I know of a couple of instances where information sent to the school was mislabeled and thrown out. So there may be a lot of schools around the country that don't even have your school's literature on file. The guidance counselor is very important in getting information to potential prospects. That's a very important person to develop communication with. And you can make an unlimited number of phone calls to the guidance counselor.

Create a Dialogue with Prospects

Another technique we use in mailing is "returns." We try to get the prospects to correspond with us. Initially, it is just a matter of having them send things back. The first thing is a questionnaire. If he sends a questionnaire back, that's good. It starts the whole process going. Another thing we send out is a questionnaire asking about summer plans. Summer plans, for us, are very important. In basketball, our major evaluation process is in July. We send forms out to prospects asking,

"Where will you be in July? What are your summer plans? Are you going to camp or summer league? What days do you play? What time?"

It helps us collect information. We also ask for a phone number, because a lot of times that can change. I think we have to be very aware of the fact that families in America are increasingly fractured. It's incredible the number of split families I encounter. So you need more than one phone number many times to stay in contact with kids. The more information you can get your prospect to send you, the better. It's very important.

So the summer plan is incredibly important to us. When we go to a camp, we like to know who is going to be there. We have a limited amount of time. We make a list of the prospects we know are going to be there. Now obviously, their schedule may change as summer goes on. But this is a way to get some idea where people are going to go. Then, of course, when the prospect sends you this information, that's a great reason for you to write back to him, telling him you appreciate knowing his summer plans. Again, you begin to develop a relationship – a dialogue.

It's vital to have your prospect involved in the process. No matter how well you know the guidance counselor, they will not release any information unless you have the prospect's permission. That's very important. So you have to get that flow of information going between you and the prospect. Those return mailings are really important, because the student has to make an effort to send it back.

You're starting to develop a relationship through the mail. When you supplement your mailings with the occasional weekly phone call, I think you can begin to really build something up.

Consistency in Recruiting

I think what probably hurts us all more than anything in recruiting is the inconsistency of our recruiting – the fact that we get hot on prospects and cold on prospects, and then get hot again because we have lost other prospects. I think the mail

basically takes the emotion out of it. You go see a kid play and you get excited about him; maybe you see him play next time, and your interest starts to wane.

Prospects are just like us. I play golf. One day I can go out and shoot 82; the next day, I might shoot 92. So if you see me shoot 82, you may think I'm a pretty good golfer. You see me shoot 92 and I'm suddenly not very good. The same thing happens to players.

We see it every summer. You only get to be in between your junior and senior year in high school one time. This is exciting. So the individual loads up. They're going everywhere and they just blow out about the 20th of July. They've been out there playing in the heat; they're traveling. These are all things they're not used to. Some of them are just flat-out homesick because they've never been away from home. They essentially go on the road for almost a month, some of these students.

> **"No matter how your prospect is playing, the mail is still rolling."**

They just absolutely self-destruct.

You may see a kid play poorly, so you may cool on his prospects. But the mail keeps rolling. He's still there; you're still mailing. You're not doing anything dramatic. We don't take a prospect off our mailing list until he commits to another school. Whether we're hot or cold on him, we don't take him off the list.

By September, he may be playing great again. That mail has still been rolling. You can only call him once a week anyway. It's not a big investment. In a lot of ways, the new rules allow you to stay involved with prospects easier than you could before. Before, if you weren't calling them a lot, then you were out of the picture.

It used to be that students would say, "I haven't heard from you guys but once a week." Once a week didn't cut it then. But now once a week is all you can do. You can stay peripherally involved with recruits without having to really make a strong commitment. I think many times you want to go "all out" early on, but prospects aren't going to make signing decisions in July. Very few of them are going to make them in September. Most students are making their decisions in October or the first of November for the early signing date.

So you have to pace yourself, so to speak. Even if you've done this with hundreds of prospects, this is *their* first time. No matter how *you* see it, it's their first time. Very few families go through recruiting more than once. Some will go through twice, but very few more than twice.

Sometimes we get to thinking of recruiting in terms of what's important to *us*. But you can't ever lose sight of the fact that we're not the ones being recruited. With the change in the rules, it's a whole different process. So it's really important to keep everybody updated and keep that mail going out – consistently.

Expect the Unexpected

Anything can happen in the springtime. Students can decide to leave your school; players can have academic problems. All of a sudden, you have a need that you did not have in the fall. You may have been recruiting all front court players, and in the springtime, you need back court players because your best player tore their anterior cruciate ligament and isn't going to play next year. Or your best player is homesick and is leaving. These things happen.

Rather than scrambling, you keep your prospecting alive with mailings. They keep reading about your school and they have some sense of what you are about. When I coached at James Madison, we were a volume recruiter. We would start out by recruiting huge numbers of prospects. We sent out our mail consistently. We had a system and it would go out like clock work.

Back in the days before early signing, there used to be an All-Star game called the Hoya Classic. I went up to see a prospect who had been on our mailing list but had never played. I said, "Wow, this kid is a terrific shooter." I got really excited about him, so I called him. His father said, "Yeah, Coach, we have all the mailings you sent us." I said, "Really?" He said, "Yeah, everything that comes in we have on file. We have yours and this other school; we have it all. We have everything that you sent us. We know all about your school."

The dad started telling *me* about our school. He'd never been there. We ended up signing this player. We did not recruit him in the purest sense of the term. We were involved with him probably for a month and he signed.

But in the larger picture, we did "recruit" him, because we made him aware of us. Then, when we really got hot on him, he was ready to do business. And he signed. We used to push hard in the fall when I was at James Madison. Many times the strategy is that everybody wants to sign prospects early. It's very difficult to do that at certain schools. The last two years I was there, we had a philosophy of never bringing a student in for a fall visit. We didn't even try. We just geared up for the spring. We used the mail. We went out to see them play. We did all our regular activities to keep people involved. Then we came on strong at the end.

The Business of Recruiting

There's a difference between doing business and recruiting. When you go in certain homes, some people you're doing business with. With other people, we're there to recruit.

> "There's a difference between doing business and recruiting."

"Will you take him if he wants to go to your school?"

When a parent or coach asks you that, they're doing business. They are ready to do business. "Will you take him if he wants to sign up tonight?" We all know the only way to answer that question. That is, unless you plan on leaving after the answer. If you say no, it's time to go. I really am surprised that more parents don't ask that question.

If I had a child who was a prospect and I was a parent, the first thing I would ask is, "Are you offering Johnny a scholarship? Now, I appreciate your interest, but this is my child we are talking about. Are you offering him a scholarship?"

If not, as a parent I'd say, "Okay, when you get ready to offer one, then you can come in my home." Because I think that way. We try not to go in anybody's home unless we're going to offer their child a scholarship. I would appreciate that courtesy if I were a parent.

You have to know your school. In a lot of schools, you're not going to sign prospects early. You're better off holding your money and sprinting at the finish line. There are a lot of good players who are still available in the springtime.

The Personal Touch in Mail

The impact of mail is a lot greater than you would think. And it's better the more personalized you can make it. I can't tell you how many college athletes I've talked to over the years who remarked about how they went to a particular school because the coach used to handwrite notes to them. I've never forgotten that. They would say, "I kept every one he sent me." I've heard that so many times. Unfortunately, I have the worst handwriting you have ever seen. So I can't do that. I just do not have good penmanship.

But if you write well and if you write legibly, that is a great asset. I think I *write* well; it's just that you can't read it. If you can write well and people can read it, it will help you recruit.

> **Send out the publications the NCAA creates. You *know* those are allowable.**

Even if you send out mass mailings, always put a handwritten note with it. "Bob, hope your week's going well." It takes a very small amount of time. Just write a little note to personalize it in some way. People really appreciate that. It's amazing how much it's appreciated.

Another good thing to send out is NCAA-generated information. The NCAA is trying to figure out a way to spend their money now, so they're sending out a lot of publications. Some of them are quite good. One of them, I remember, focused on the new academics. It had the whole scale in there with grade point averages and SAT and ACT correlations. These are very good things to be sending out to prospects.

We sometimes order a hundred of them and just send them out to all our prospects. It's an NCAA publication. It is allowable by the NCAA rules to send it out. It's very informative and you can obviously just send along a note, "Here, Tommy, I thought this was something you and your parents would enjoy looking at." We're very interested in keeping everybody informed about new things.

You can have an advantage by sending out these publications. Getting this information out is really important. It's something that you are allowed to do according to the rules. If I'm a parent and I receive this from a school, I have to feel good about that. I have to think that school has a real interest in my son or daughter, academically speaking.

What else can you send out? Questionnaires. Postcards have to be of a generic nature now, but are still a good thing to send, particularly in the month of July.

And notecards. In basketball, we're running around watching a lot of these recruits play. We have notecards. We'll go see a prospect play. We'll just write a little note, "Dear Johnny, enjoyed seeing you play today." Sometimes we'll give it to the coach and ask him to give it to the player, which is, in a way, using the mail.

We do that on various occasions, if it's appropriate. You can also send the notecards in the mail. Just send a note from where you are. You may be watching the recruit play in Los Angeles in the Slam-and-Jam Tournament and you just write, "Enjoyed seeing you play."

Send the postcard and by the time he gets it, you're somewhere else. He will be back home and realize you were there. It's a recruiting technique to use the mail to show your presence. It just shows the recruit you're interested in him.

The Little Things

Other things you can send include a media guide or recruiting brochure; one or the other. Also, promotional handbills, wallet-size schedule cards or a summer camp brochure.

> **"Make sure your letters don't try to do all things."**

Try to personalize the notes you write; use nicknames. Find out what the recruit likes to be called. Don't refer to him as Robert if his nickname is Bobby. And make sure your letters don't try to do all things. Stick to one theme per letter.

Mailings to parents and coaches are very important. There is an estimate that 75 percent of the mailings you send should not be about your sport. They should be about academics. One out of four should relate to the sport; the other three should be about the university, the campus community and life in general.

The mail is a great equalizer. It will help you reach prospects that you probably wouldn't reach without the mail. Use the mail to your advantage and see what kind of a positive effect it has on your ability to recruit.

Author Profile: Ernie Nestor

Ernie Nestor is assistant men's basketball coach at Wake Forest University. The former head coach at George Mason University has 23 years of college recruiting experience. A graduate of Alderson-Broaddus College in West Virginia, his other coaching stops include James Madison University and the University of California-Berkeley. He also served as head coach of the United States Jones Cup team in 1996.

Division II Championship Recruiting Methods

by Ken Shields

A recruit doesn't care how much you know; they want to know how much you care.

That statement says a lot about today's recruits and athletes in general. I think parents, to a large extent, certainly take on that disposition as well. There's a tremendous number of things that go into being a successful recruiter. One of the key variables is if a prospect and his or her parents are truly convinced of the genuineness, sincerity and caring of the head coach and his or her staff.

Parents love their children very, very much and they want them to be happy. They want them to be successful. So naturally, they want their child to be in the hands of someone whom they're very comfortable with.

I believe it's important to always remember to be yourself. It's much easier to be yourself than to be someone else. I subscribe to the theory that we "learn from everyone, but imitate no one." In coaching, this means learning from other coaches we have worked with. I believe "the apple doesn't fall far from the tree." We are what we've been exposed to...but you still have to be yourself. You can't be phony.

One of the greatest compliments I've ever received was when one of my assistant coaches at Northern Kentucky University told someone, "You don't work *for* Ken Shields, you work *with* Ken Shields."

What Parents Want to Know

When you make a presentation, you should accentuate the positive and somewhat camouflage the negative. If you have confidence in your university or college and you feel good about the academics offered, you are going to emphasize that. That may mean highlighting the majors that are offered. You need to know whether you can provide something that a recruit is interested in. A lot of parents want to know your school's pupil-to-teacher ratio. At our institution, we don't have graduate assistants who teach. Our faculty basically encompasses professors.

But on the negative side, we have a lot of part-time instructors. This is just one example of how you want to tell the truth, but you'll want to emphasize the more positive aspect.

Parents also like to know whether your school is accredited and what the status is of the department their son or daughter is most interested in. This is a good time to seek out someone with some expertise in that department and line up a session with them during the recruit's visit. When a recruit doesn't have a good idea of the field they'd like to pursue, you can use the academic coordinator in your area.

Seeing Is Believing

Visibility is significant to many recruits. Playing on television can be the difference between getting – and not getting – a recruit. The Division II national championship basketball game is played at 1:00 in the afternoon, just prior to the Division I semifinal games. If you're playing in that game, a lot of people are seeing your school. We had a young man from Florida, who lived in North Carolina, who saw us on television. That was important to him. He had opportunities to visit a lot of places, but he remembered seeing us on TV and that was the difference for him.

> "If you can, use proximity as an advantage of choosing your school."

Some players are looking for a high-profile school as their ticket to the professional leagues. We know that 99.9 percent of Division II and Division III players are not going to play professionally. Obviously, a student-athlete who chooses Division II or III is interested in other things besides playing professionally. That doesn't mean that they don't dream it will happen. Scottie Pippen played Division II basketball. But there's not a whole lot of other examples. Some players choose Division I as a road to expedite their introduction to the NBA and becoming a multi-millionaire. We don't have those kinds of connections.

Something that also makes a difference is the proximity of your university to the recruit's home. We seem to be getting away from the time when young people wanted to "get away" to now they feel they want to stay close to home.

If you're in a situation where you're recruiting someone from your area, you must really highlight the advantages of coming to your school. I stress everything from the fact that their name is going to be in the newspaper to their post-playing days when they'll have instant name recognition in the job market.

I also sell to local players that they won't be spending their money on travel and they won't waste a lot of time commuting. Plus, their phone bills won't be as high, either. If you're dealing with an athlete who doesn't come from a whole lot, those factors are tremendously important.

Playing the Role of Parent

Most of us who have been in the coaching profession any length of time know how easy it is to become close with an athlete. The great UCLA basketball coach John Wooden always said, "In coaching, we don't necessarily *like* every player we have, but we do *love* every player that we have."

I think the idea of love is important. In my entire career as a basketball coach, I've never sent a team onto the floor before a game without saying, "God bless you" and "I love you." And every time I say it, I mean it. I tell my prospects that I will not dehumanize them. I will not scream at them in front of people and embarrass them, myself, the school, or their family and friends. Likewise, they should never do the same to me or a member of my staff. I believe a coach is a teacher first and foremost. You teach players what to do, then let them play. For me, this means not having to yell at them every time up and down the basketball court.

What Players Want to Know

Some recruits are interested in the size of the crowds at our games. They also like to know about our facilities. Some players want to play in a larger facility. They are also interested in your weight room. Recruits oftentimes are curious about what their future teammates are like. Parents like to know this as well. I like to expose recruits to my crème de la crème, or the cream of the crop. It's important the prospective athlete get a feel for the players, their value system and how they function.

Prospects also take an interest in the coaching staff – and not just the head coach. The assistant coaches do a lot of the early recruiting, so this is a good time to establish good rapport. As a head coach, it's important to delegate duties to different members of your staff. They're the people who will be involved with phone calls, NCAA rules and regulations and nearly everything else that goes into the recruiting process. My assistant coaches are integrally involved in every aspect and obviously the players recognize that as well.

> **"Prospects want to get to know your whole coaching staff – not just you."**

Players also want to know about your team's style of play. There's a saying in basketball that if you're an up-tempo team and you're not winning, fans will stay patient longer than if you're using a methodical, controlled style of offense and losing. We encourage them to come and watch us play if they can. It's also an opportunity for them to see how we treat our athletes.

No matter what sport you coach or the style of your team's play, recruits want to know how you'll treat them.

I'm a great believer you catch more flies with honey than you do with vinegar. As a coach, I also believe you have to have confidence in your players. In basketball, for example, you don't have to be running up and down the sidelines, stomping your feet. You're a teacher first and foremost. You teach what you are doing and then you let them go play. You intervene if they need additional guidance. But you have to let them learn. I tell my assistants, "They can't hear you anyway if they are at the other end of the floor. You're just talking to yourself."

There are some big-time coaches that are somewhat enamored of themselves and they are more worried about being seen than doing their job. Players will be able to tell what kind of a coach you are if they can see you in a game situation. The way that you work with players in a competition will give players an idea of how they will be treated – and that's what they want to know.

The Loyalty Factor

We all know the significance of loyalty. In my career as a head coach – 23 years as a high school head coach and 11 years as a collegiate head coach – I've been fortunate enough to have my teams win well over 600 games. I know that my assistant coaches played a key role in that success, as well as the players who actually played and won each and every game.

> **"The loyalty factor extends to every athlete you make contact with."**

The loyalty factor must extend to each and every athlete you make contact with in the recruiting process. Sometimes, you'll lose a recruit because they have a girlfriend who's strongly influencing their decision. When something like this happens, it can obviously be frustrating. But I go to great strides to end our "courtship" on a positive note. If you've departed on good terms, it may pay off in the long run. I like to send them on their way on a positive note. I might say, "Good luck. We sure would have loved to have had you as a player. If the day comes that for some reason you want to come back, call me." To be successful at the Division II and Division III level, you need to have players who transfer out of Division I programs. You never know when the day will come that they change their mind and want to come to your school.

Relating to the Parents

Sometimes the player is the key in the ultimate decision, because most of the time, the parents will go along with the player's preference. But not all the time. Many times, the most important person you need to convince is the mom.

Former Marquette basketball coach Al McGuire used to say if he could get in the kitchen with a recruit's mom, he had the deal sealed. I'm from the same mold. I'm very comfortable in a kitchen and believe that this is a way to relate to a recruit's mother. During home visits, mom is key. Mothers want to feel good about who they're entrusting their son or daughter to and they want to know what lies in store for them as well.

When we recruited LaRon Moore, an All-American who played four fabulous years with us, I really felt that the turning point in us getting him was his mom. She felt good about him coming to our university and working with our staff. The fact that they could drive an hour and 15 minutes to see him play didn't hurt. Moms want to see the dormitory. They want to see the rooms. They are interested in where their children are going to be staying.

What moms want to know and what dads want to know are two very different things. Dads want to know how much publicity their son or daughter will receive or what their chances are of significant playing time. So many times fathers live their lives through the athletic life of their child. This can create a problem. I ask my players what their fathers do. Then I tell them, "I coach for a living." That usually sets the tone for criticism from parents.

I don't like to make a home visit unless I'm convinced I'm going to make an offer to that athlete. If I'm not convinced I'm going to make an offer, I don't go on the visit. I want to be able to say, "Hey, we want you, this is what we're dealing with." Of course, I realize it's different with Division III. My son played Division III football and there was a tremendous amount of help which came to him, to a large extent due to his academic situation.

The Luck Factor

Something very, very important in the whole realm of recruiting is luck. We have made mistakes. What happens is that sometimes when athletes get to college, they lose their competitive hearts. They get interested in fraternities or working. I look back on years when we went 8-16

> **"Part of recruiting success is luck – pure and simple."**

and I think we had some wonderful players during those years, but they wanted to cut grass and make money. Or they wanted to play softball four or five times a week. They had other things on their minds. They weren't willing to attend summer school and try to help themselves out academically. And, more importantly, they didn't want to spend time in the weight room or do the things that you do to be successful in basketball.

The role of the head coach is similar to that of a closing pitcher in baseball or a good salesperson. You have to have the ability to pull it all together in the end. Everybody is different. Motivation is a big factor in getting athletes' attention and then tuning them in to your program. Self-motivation is a key type of motivation.

The key to successful recruiting is to be able to find the "hot spots" which will motivate a prospect into believing in your system and your school. I use "love motivation." If a player knows how much you care, they'll buy into your genuineness. I think you can tell that it works by how many players come back or call you on the phone. The yardstick is whether they come back or keep in touch.

The Home Visit

Whenever possible, I believe in taking along one of my assistant coaches on a home visit. They're an integral part of your team and it's important that the athlete and his or her parents get to know your staff.

When we went on the home recruiting visit to see LaRon Moore, I invited one of my minority assistant coaches to go along. Unfortunately, he had a prior commitment and declined.

After that visit, I was criticized by some people on campus because our minority coach did not tag along. They felt that would keep LaRon from coming. But it didn't, obviously. His decision was heavily influenced by his mother, Nancy, and his high school coach. His high school coach was very much involved with the visit. He was very impressed with us and that's something to keep in mind. A lot of times, high school coaches don't like to get involved in the recruiting decision because they don't want to be blamed. Other high school coaches just aren't interested. If you are working with junior college coaches, they often have their own recruiting to do. But having coaches involved – if they want to be involved – can be very helpful.

There are many rules and regulations for recruiting which must be followed closely, no matter what level your school is competing on. Make sure you and your coaching staff are aware of the rules and how to abide by them.

Networking

One thing I was missing when I started coaching in college after a long high school career, was networking. When I accepted the job at Northern Kentucky University after all those years of coaching high school, I instantly realized I didn't have a collegiate network of contacts. I had a tremendous high school network in place, but it wasn't helping.

> **"The longer you are in coaching, the more your network will help you."**

I hired one of my former players to serve as my part-time assistant coach. He had been a high school coach himself, but he didn't have any collegiate networking contacts, either. Not having those contacts really hurt our recruiting that year. Like any good businessman, it's important to establish a strong network of contacts.

Of course, the longer you are in coaching, the more you are apt to have networking work to your advantage.

Instinct Versus Talent

You have to have athletes with talent. If you don't, you're not going to win. I tell young people, "All of us have the same capacity to hustle. But we all have different talents." Our skill or talent level was decided in the bedroom when we were conceived. Intellectual skill, physical strength – it was all decided way back then. I believe that we have certain instinctual talents and we have cerebral talents. If you have great instinctual talent, but you're missing cerebral skills, you are not going to be what you could be. And vice versa.

One year, we had probably the most talented instinctual player that I ever coached. But we had to let him go because he didn't have the discipline and he didn't cooperate. That was a shame, because he was a tremendous player, as far as talent. Our talent comes from God. What we do with it is our gift back to God.

Timeliness and Organization Are Keys to Success

Be organized. I'm a great believer in having your practice schedule written up. I'm also a great believer in my assistants having copies of the schedule. I like to have the schedule on the wall by lunchtime so the players can see it. Of course, you have the right to change that at any time if you so choose. But you should stay with your schedule unless you are immediately preparing for a team.

> **"I believe in being where you are supposed to be, when you are supposed to be there."**

I'm a great believer in starting everything on an "off minute." We never start practice at 3:20 or 3:30. We'll start practice at 3:23 or 3:33, for example. If we have an early practice session, I like to say the bus is leaving at 1:59 or 2:01, not 2:00. I believe that people respond better. Players know about being on time.

I believe in being where you're supposed to be when you're supposed to be there. I get up at a quarter to five in the morning and I look forward to it.

Being a Role Model for Players

If you do what you like, you'll like what you do. I've been blessed by Almighty God, not only with a lovely wife and a fine family of five children and three grandchildren, but I've been blessed with my health. In all my years as a teacher and as a coach, I've missed just one day of work, and that was for surgery.

I'm a great believer that Almighty God needs to be numero uno in all our lives and that family is second.

I always encourage young people, our players, to tell their parents that they love them. I think that's important. I never speak at a camp that I don't say, "Please go home and tell your parents that you love them."

John Wooden once said that every day that we live our lives we should try to do something nice for somebody else without ever expecting something in return. It might be a hello, a phone call, just talking to somebody, or taking them to lunch.

Coach Wooden also said that "the smallest gift is larger than the greatest thought." How many times do we think we want to do something for someone? It might be a note or a phone call, but we forget to do it.

I've always tried to do something about it. I'm not a perfect person, but what you see is what you get.

Summary

I really believe that you have to be a good teacher first and foremost. You should be yourself, be prepared and be prepared to fail.

As John Wooden used to say, "Failure to prepare is to prepare to fail." You must be organized. Develop a game plan for recruiting and stick with it.

In athletics, you have to have a competitive heart. You have to have great work habits. You have to be able to make good decisions on and off the floor. You have to be persistent.

Panel Profile: Ken Shields

Ken Shields is the head men's basketball coach at Northern Kentucky University. The National Coach-of-the-Year award winner has 11 years of college recruiting experience and is regarded as one of the top recruiters in NCAA Division II. His Norse teams are perennial national championship contenders.

STRATEGIES FOR JUNIOR COLLEGE THROUGH DIVISION I RECRUITING

by Steve Silvey

A lot of coaches are self-taught recruiters. I know when I left the high school ranks, right after the 1984 Olympic Games, I went to Texas A&M University and nobody really knew what I should do. Right off the bat, my boss, Charlie Thomas, the renowned track coach who retired in 1990, told me that the key to being a great college coach is, first and foremost, to be able to recruit. So I gave that some serious thought when trying to learn how to recruit, and what methods I should use.

I believe that the early bird catches the worm. There are hundreds of universities out there that are trying to retain the services of a particular blue-chip athlete. Sometimes, the schools that are first into the home or the first to make that phone contact are the ones that are going to be the winners.

Just as there are many ways to skin a cat, there are many ways to recruit. What that means is that you have to be yourself, find out which method works best for you and run with it.

The way I learned to recruit was just a compilation of things that I picked up by talking to other coaches. I have a sign that I put in my office when I got to the University of Arkansas a couple of years ago. It says, "Great teams are produced by great recruiting." I know a lot of times, coaches get caught up in how good a coach they are. The bottom line is you have to have the talent available to you to coach. If you're going to be successful and have a winning program, you have to have the talent you need – and that comes from recruiting. So I have a sign in my office just to remind me of the simple fact that recruiting is the key.

I was talking to a coach about recruiting at the NCAA Division I national track championships in Eugene, Oregon. He said, "The first thing you had better bring is a telephone." It's the truth. If you're going to be a great recruiter, you had better plan on living on that telephone and being accessible by telephone whenever somebody needs to talk to you.

The Recruiting Cycle

In my book, recruiting is never done. It always cycles through. Whether you're finished now or not, you're still building for next year. So I really don't see that there's ever a down period in recruiting.

I know from the track and field standpoint, we have the cross-country season in the fall and then we have track and field starting in January. We might sign people for letters of intent in August, but we'll also always be trying to find new talent to bring in the first of January before indoor track season begins. Our recruiting season never ends. We're always on the phone. We're always trying to find talent.

First of all, when we talk about recruiting, I don't want to leave out the junior colleges. Right now, it's a lot easier to recruit at the junior college level because of the very stringent academic requirements set by the NCAA. Athletes that were considered good students before the stricter NCAA academic standards are now considered marginal and might not even get in. So the talent pool for a junior college is very abundant. It's probably so overabundant that it's almost hard to find schools for all the athletes.

> **"As a junior college coach, I would have athletes who didn't have a dime of scholarship money."**

But at the junior college level, you can maximize. I know as a junior college coach, you can use a lot of federal grant money that isn't available for the NCAA schools. At the NCAA level, we're allowed to use Pell Grants, but at the junior college level we were able to use SEOG and Pell Grants. Every year I prided myself on trying to pick up athletes that were from low-income families. A lot of times, I had as many as 10 or 15 of the athletes on my junior college team that didn't have a dime of scholarship money because federal grant money took care of everything.

Grant money can really help you stretch your scholarship money by getting low-income athletes in your program who qualify for federal grant money that you cannot use at the NCAA levels.

The Numbers Game

Bill Bergan, who was a very successful track coach at Iowa State University, told me a long time ago that recruiting is like insurance sales. Basically, if you contact 10 people, you might sell to two or three people. If you contact 100 people, you might sell to 20 or 30 people. The more people you contact, the more successful you are going to be.

As recruiters, we win some battles and we lose some battles. That's part of life. You have to be prepared for that. You're not going to get every athlete that you want. One year, I had the top hurdler in the United States committed to the University of Arkansas a couple of weeks before signing. The next thing I knew, he decided not to come to the University of Arkansas because he was going to another school with his best friend. That's part of the game. We wanted to have him, but it didn't work out.

If you've been recruiting for a while, you've probably had some unbelievable things happen to you. I had a situation in my early years when I was at Texas A&M, back about 1987. The University of Texas-El Paso had their track program sanctioned by the NCAA and they were going to be put on probation for three years. They were going to let all of their athletes transfer out. Well, it just so happened there was a 27'2" long jumper there named Tyrus Jefferson. At this point at Texas A&M, we almost had a potential NCAA championship track program and we felt if we could bring in this one last person in January, we might be able to win the NCAA track championship.

I went in mid-December to Tyrus Jefferson's dorm room at the University of Texas-El Paso. I was at his dorm room at 10:00 p.m. the night before the signing period. He committed to me. He said, "Coach, I'll sign with you tomorrow morning. I will be a part of the Texas A&M program." Then, the phone rang. It was Mike Conley, an assistant coach at the University of Arkansas. Mike is the 1992 Olympic triple jump champion. He called Tyrus while I was in the dorm room. Tyrus said to him, "It looks like I'm going to Texas A&M, because the Texas A&M coach is here in my room right now." I thought, "Yes, I got this one. There's no way that Mike Conley can beat me because he's in Fayetteville, Arkansas, and I'm right here in El Paso, Texas."

> **"In recruiting, there are no sure things."**

I left that night, very happy about the situation. The next morning at 8 o'clock, I'm on his doorstep. Tyrus opens the door. The lights are off. I go in, and all of a sudden, I realize there's an extra body in the room. The lights come on and there's Mike Conley, the University of Arkansas assistant coach, in the room. I'm thinking, "How in the heck did he get here? He was talking to the young man at 10 last night from Fayetteville (Arkansas)." He ended up driving to Tulsa right after he got off the phone. He got on a 6:30 a.m. flight, got into El Paso at 7:45, rushed to the campus and beat me to the room.

This was an ugly experience. I was expecting to sign this young man, bring him in at mid-semester and possibly win the NCAA championship. Instead, it turned into a competition between me and Mike Conley, a renowned nine-time NCAA champion. We both were in the room. Need I say more?

Tyrus was very confused, and Mike made a suggestion. He said, "Why don't we both leave and give him an hour to think about it?" So we both left the dorm room. At first, we were watching each other. Then, I went down the street to a pay phone. I called my boss and said, "Mike Conley is here and he's causing all kinds of confusion." Then right around the corner, here comes Mike Conley, when I'm cussing him out. But Mike, I guess, in that hour time frame, sneaked back in and signed Tyrus. I learned a valuable lesson. There are no sure things.

It just shows that you have things happen to you as a recruiter – and they are sometimes strange. You have to have an open mind. I'm certain that sometimes you're going to get the upper hand and sometimes you're going to lose. But that's the whole thing. It's just like sales. You're not going to be able to sell to everybody. Somebody's going to turn you down. But, the odds are that someone's going to buy from you. That's the thing that you have to keep an open mind about, that if you contact enough people, and you work hard enough, you are going to be successful. You're going to win more times than you lose.

If you're going to be in college athletics, you cannot be afraid to work 70 to 80 hours a week if you want to be successful. I've been very fortunate that I've been associated with winning teams every level I've been at, whether it's Division I or junior college. It's like a very successful assistant coach at Texas A&M once told me: "If you can recruit, you can be a hellacious sales person." Because that's what you're doing. You're selling your university. That's what it's all about.

Positivity Will Win Out

Always sell the positives of your program. There are people who have nothing better to do than to negative recruit and that's going to come back and haunt them.

> **"Negative recruiting will come back to haunt you."**

I know in some conferences they have rules and regulations that prohibit negative recruiting or you will be reprimanded. My boss at Texas A&M in the mid-80s, Charlie Thomas, said, "Always sell your positives." That's very important. If you have to lower yourself to these other coaches' levels, don't. Those aren't the schools that are winning. They think that's going to help them, but it's not.

Always be honest and sell the positives about your program: what things you've done, what your school has done, how your program's improving, and things like that. I think it is sometimes overlooked, but you're not going to go wrong by selling the positives of your program.

One year, we tried to double team with our football people in recruiting certain two-sport athletes. The first thing one of the football staff members said was "We can't get that guy; he's in the University of Texas' backyard." You can't take that approach. *Anybody* can be recruited *anywhere* in the country if you keep an open mind. Some of the prospects I thought I would never sign because they were in the backyard of another major university, I signed anyway. Don't let geography get in your way. That's something you have to keep an open mind about.

It's not easy, but somebody who grew up around the University of Texas might be ready for a change. I've seen lots of kids from Florida choose schools in colder-weather climates. I guess sometimes people get sick of the sunshine and the beach and the water, and they want to head north. Sometimes they are in such a perfect environment for so long that it becomes just another place to live, and they want to expand their horizons and go somewhere else (geographically) in the United States to go to school. So you have to have an open mind. I've taken a lot of players out of other schools' backyards when I thought I would never sign them.

Network!

As coaches and recruiters, we have to have good contacts. You have to establish a recruiting base of successful high school coaches, whether it's in your state or throughout the country. I know if I need to find information about somebody in Los Angeles, I can call a couple of coaches and they'll tell me in a heartbeat. Having coached in the state of Texas for 13 years, I can call somebody in Houston or Dallas and get them to send me articles or weekly stat sheets or whatever's in the newspapers. I think it's important that you have good contacts that you can use. Maybe it's not this year or two years down the line or three years, but someday it will be a great thing to have at your disposal.

That may mean sending them a Christmas card to let them know that you want to keep in contact with them on recruiting. Or if you have some summer camps and you want them on your camp staff, something like that can build a relationship with those high school coaches and help generate interest in your program.

We have two or three of the top high school coaches in Arkansas, who if they find anybody who looks good, they're going to call us and let us know. I think it's important to build that type of recruiting base to help you.

Another thing Charlie Thomas told me was, "You need to have something about your school in front of that recruit once a week." So, when I was at Texas A&M, I was putting together a newsletter or article or some sort of information about Texas A&M and mailing it to them once a week. When I was at Blinn Junior College, I would probably send out 200-300 mail-outs a week and I was the one licking the envelopes. I also sent mailings to certain media people and other coaches as part of my recruiting base.

Some of the other coaches probably look at me and say, "That guy's crazy. Every week he sends out 125 mail-outs." Well, at Arkansas, we have a great tradition,

but other schools are challenging us on the national level, so we have to upgrade our recruiting tools. I send out things about the track team, or the school in general, or about our other sports programs.

I know there are lots of recruiting services out there. But you have to find out what works for you. If you know your fellow coaches in the profession, talk to them. They will give you some ideas. There are some sources out there that are junk. They just want your money. Then there are other sources out there that are very good. You really need to invest time in finding good ones that will meet your needs.

Even if your school won't pay, some of these things you may need to pay for out of your own pocket. I know as a junior college coach, I had to buy a fax machine and a computer. I had to pay for publications. That was part of the game. You can write many of these expenses off on your income tax. If you have to go somewhere to recruit a player and your school doesn't reimburse you, some of these expenses can also be written off.

Find the Recruit's Key Person

> **The key person might not always be the person you would expect.**

Find the person who the recruit turns to for advice. It could be a parent, a brother, a cousin, a high school teammate or coach. We talk a lot with the football recruiters at our school, because they have 95 scholarships and we have 12. So we need as much help as we can get. One time, they were talking about how they had just signed one of the top fifty high school football players in Texas. The coaches were telling me that they got to know the student's guidance counselor, and the guidance counselor was one of the most influential persons in this athlete's life. They worked and worked the guidance counselor and they signed the athlete. Texas A&M still can't understand why they didn't sign the player. But our coaches said it was the guidance counselor. That was the key.

Never count out anybody, because it could be any one of a number of individuals who is the key to getting that athlete. This guidance counselor was always making sure that athletes were taking care of academics and going to class. The athlete really had a lot of respect for his guidance counselor. We were trying to recruit some track athletes from the same high school. We found the same thing. Two or three other athletes confided in this guidance counselor more than they did with their families. That guidance counselor really must be a neat person.

Look for "Sleeper" Recruits

Don't overlook the sleeper recruit. You've probably recruited some of the best athletes in the country. Maybe a top 10 athlete or a McDonald's All-American or a high school All-American. Many times some of those players don't turn out to be the college athlete that they were built up to be. That's the great thing about recruiting a sleeper, somebody who hasn't been overcoached or from a high school that doesn't have a marquee program, because the expectations are low.

To give you an example, in 1994 (my last year at a junior college) I recruited a sprinter out of South Carolina. His name was Timmy Montgomery. He was a 10.61 (100-meter dash) high school sprinter. He came from a high school that was so small they couldn't even run a sprint relay with four people because they didn't have four people on the track team.

They didn't even have a real track. They had a dirt track.

He won state as a junior. The next year, in our program, he ran 9.96 (electronically timed); that was a world junior record. That was quite an accomplishment. This kid was probably not a top 50 high school sprinter in the country, but all of a sudden he had the fastest 100 meters ever run by an athlete 19 years of age or younger in the sport of track and field. The guy was only about 5'10" and about 128 pounds soaking wet. We called him "Slim-Fast" because he was so skinny. It was just one of those things that as a coach you can take a lot of satisfaction in.

I've coached elite athletes who were national high school record holders and number one ranked high school athletes of the year. A lot of those guys were a pain in the butt to coach. They think they've done it all in high school, they're "god's gift to sports," and you can't tell them anything because they've already done so many great things before you've even started working with them. That's why it's rewarding having sleepers that just come out of nowhere, who develop and get better and better. You take a lot of satisfaction because that is part of coaching, too.

I think from a coaching standpoint this is another way of maximizing your dollars by investing a little bit of money on a diamond-in-the-rough and letting him develop. You might get a lot for your scholarship dollar. I think that's something that we can't lose sight of.

Honesty First

I feel honesty is the best policy in recruiting. Unfortunately, there are many coaches out there who lie to recruits and parents. One legendary track coach was talking to an athlete's parents, and the player's dad asked him, "Are there some good churches in the community?" The coach replied, "Oh yes, sir. In fact, every Sunday morning I pick up the athletes. I drive the church bus. I come by and I pick them up at the dorm and I personally take them to church." That coach probably doesn't have the faintest clue what church is all about, but he literally told the parents that he drove the church bus.

> **"One coach lied to a prospect's parents and told him he drove the bus to church."**

Integrity is also important. Don't abuse your power. We had this policy when I was coaching in junior college, that anytime we had a Division I coach come to our campus around noon time, we could provide them with a free meal. But there was this one coach who abused this. Every week, one of our administrators would see this same Division I coach eating in our cafeteria – for free. We nicknamed him "Free Lunch." It got so bad that the school had to implement a policy that we had to have prior approval before Division I coaches could eat free in the junior college cafeteria, because this one Division I coach abused the policy.

It is very important that you are honest with the athletes. If I'm asked a question I can't answer, I'll say, "I don't know." I'm a firm believer in "honesty is the best policy." When I go into a recruit's home, I tell it like it is. I'm not going to give them a bunch of lies, because if I lie to get an athlete to come to my school, and then they get there and find out it's not true, what's going to happen? They're probably going to leave. They're sure going to be upset. I don't benefit if they leave the campus because I lied to get them there. They don't benefit either. We waste time, energy and money. So honesty is the best policy.

You see this happen over and over again. I've heard schools tell a recruit, "We've got an all-weather track." So an athlete who has never visited the campus signs with them. One recruit from Michigan went down to a Texas junior college and he said to the coach, "I thought you said we had an all-weather track." The coach replied, "We do. It's a dirt track. It's muddy when it's wet. It's hard when it's sunny." He lied to this kid and the recruit ended up leaving after only one semester. He was a very talented athlete.

Paint a True Picture

You hear so much about lying during recruiting. I think it comes back to haunt you. I really believe that honesty is your best policy. Tell them how it is. A lot of athletes are concerned about graduation rates. I know they're caught up in the

> **"It's important to paint a realistic picture for your athletes. I think they will respect you more for it."**

figures, but I tell them how it is, that we can give them tutorial help and academic monitoring, but the two things we can't do for an athlete are go to class for them and study for them. Sometimes athletes think you're going to "take care of them" academically and that's not the case. It's very important that you paint a realistic picture because I think they'll respect you more. Hopefully that athlete will take it to heart.

When I was an athlete coming out of high school, I had coaches tell me, "Come to my school and we'll go to Arizona or Florida for spring break." Well, I went to one of those schools and we never went on a spring track trip. So I sympathize with athletes who are being lied to.

I think the bottom line is, "Is it worth breaking a rule to jeopardize your career and your family?" With governing bodies like the Junior College Athletic Association or the NCAA, once you've broken recruiting rules, you can be marked for life. It's not worth it. If it means you could lose your job, it's not worth it.

It can affect your future employment. With a major track job I heard about, the first thing they were looking for was applicants who were completely clean with the NCAA. Applicants were asked, "Have you ever had a violation? Have you been reprimanded by your institution?" That's one of the prerequisites. Anybody who was called in to interview for that position could not have a mark on their resumé. The program was under NCAA sanctions and if they had another problem, that program would get the death penalty by the NCAA. Keep that in mind. It's not worth breaking a rule to get a blue-chip athlete.

Recruiting Internationally

If you want to recruit internationally, you have to build recruiting contacts. Sometimes these recruiting contacts take time. It might take two or three years before you can even see any type of benefit.

> **"If you can help athletes to get an education, it will lead you to getting other athletes."**

When I first was at Texas A&M, I tried to recruit some Jamaican athletes. Finally, I took a vacation to Jamaica and I met some people first-hand. The dividends didn't happen overnight, but over the next year or two, I started seeing some results. In my seven years at Blinn Junior College, I was fortunate enough to coach about 27 Jamaican athletes who were recruited as a result of those contacts.

If you can help their athletes to get a quality education and help them to improve as an athlete, that is a positive experience for them. In turn, it will lead you to getting other athletes. But it takes time. It's very important that you are open minded. If you can meet with these people first-hand, it helps.

If you're serious about getting some international contacts in your sport, I would visit international competitions. Bring along recruiting materials and try to meet with some of the federations. That means going and knocking on the door and trying to meet the head of the Brazilian federation for basketball operations. Even one contact can be successful.

At the British Commonwealth championship in Vancouver in 1994, there were athletes there with all their documentation ready, and their suitcases packed. A lot of those athletes had no intention of going back to their countries after the British Commonwealth championships. They were looking for someone to find them and offer them a scholarship to come to the United States.

I wasn't there, but another friend of mine who was a coach at a Division II school told me that he made some good contacts. In fact, two players signed within the next week or two, because they had all their academic paperwork in line and were ready to search out an American institution.

Sometimes, as recruiters, you have to be at the right place at the right time. You need to be at a world basketball championship or the world swimming championships or the Olympic Games or the PanAmerican Games. In track and field, we try to be at the World Junior Track and Field Championships.

As coaches, we get criticized for not developing some of the American talent. When I was at the junior college level, I had a hard time signing great Texas athletes. The school I was at was not a household name. If I couldn't get the Texas athletes, I had to go get the best athletes in the United States. If I couldn't get those, then I had to recruit internationally. I would bring in seven or eight international players to tie into my program.

International Athlete is a Positive Force

International players are very positive role models for your teams. They sometimes come from countries that are very poor financially. The opportunity to come to the United States is like gold. If they can leave the United States with a four-year education and go back home, they're set for life. International athletes are some of the most outstanding people I've ever met in my lifetime. They're the ones that I have no hesitation about bringing in my home for Thanksgiving or Christmas, because they are such a neat type of person that they appreciate what you're doing for them.

I've had a couple of them come up to me and say, "Coach, I don't understand how come this guy here from the U.S. doesn't want to go to class; he doesn't want to make his grades." They think of this as a golden opportunity for their success later in life. I think having an international athlete or two on your team is a very positive learning experience for the rest of your athletes. Especially if you have athletes who have dreams of being in the Olympics or competing on an international level.

> **"I first try to develop U.S. athletes, but if I can't find what I need here, I look internationally."**

I don't think you can go wrong by making international contacts. It might take time and money, but see if you can work a vacation around going to Jamaica or to Australia or Europe. You can make some really good contacts. My personal philosophy is try to develop the U.S. athletes first, but if you can't find what you need here in the United States, you might have to go the international route to get those athletes.

The International Recruiting Process

The best thing to do if you're trying to recruit internationally, is to first call the country's embassy in the Washington, D.C. area. They will give you the name of a person you can contact in that respective country and then you can send a package and a letter of introduction about your school. That's basically how it starts. You have to have an address. Calling the embassy for that particular country is the best way to start the process.

Second, if you're at a competition and you know that a team has a Russian player or a Caribbean athlete or an athlete from South America, get to know that player, before the match or after the match. A lot of times they may not like the particular school they're at or that particular coach, or they might be able to turn you on to athletes from their country that they would recommend. It might be someone they know who is good back home or some young, emerging athlete.

Finally, if you have an international athlete in your program and you treat him well and he responds to your coaching, he will help to turn you on to other athletes. These athletes are your best diplomat for the future in recruiting. If they get a degree from your school, they usually go back home and tell everyone they know. It might take time, but when you make contact with an athlete or coach an athlete, it might be your ticket to success for the next 10, 15 or 20 years, whenever you need a good international athlete.

Remember, great teams are made from championship recruiting efforts. No matter how good the coach tries to be, you're only going to be so good without having great recruiting classes. And finally, the early bird catches the worm. Be honest, be open, be yourself. Follow the rules of the NCAA or the Junior College Athletic Association. And always sell the positive facts of your program.

Author Profile: Steve Silvey

Steve Silvey is assistant men's track coach at the University of Arkansas. The winningest coach in junior college history, with 15 national titles while at Blinn Junior College, he has produced national and international track champions. In addition to Blinn, other coaching stops include Texas A&M University and the Zambian Olympic track team.

Division III Championship Recruiting Methods

by Jeff Swenson

Augsburg College has 1,500 students. We're a small private liberal arts college located in the heart of the Minneapolis/St. Paul (MN) area. As is common in most athletic departments at the Division III level, our staff positions are really varied. We wear a lot of hats and we have a lot of responsibilities.

I'm the head wrestling coach. I'm also an assistant athletic director, in charge of eligibility for all the men's sports. I'm responsible for transportation and lodging for all the men's sports. I also direct our athletic alumni base of about 2,000 people and I produce a newsletter that goes out six times a year. In addition to that, I'm also the strength coach and assistant football coach. However, I only recruit for wrestling. My football duties only include the "on-the-field, day-to-day" operations of the football program, and only during the football season.

Considering all the positions and responsibilities I have, we have a very focused recruiting plan that is very systematic. Because of my different job responsibilities, I don't have the opportunity to do some of the things that other schools do. That's probably true for most Division III coaches.

NCAA Division III rules are very different from Division I. We have no signing dates. There are no letters of intent. There is no Proposition 48. There is no NCAA clearinghouse to go through and there are no athletic scholarships. There are also no limitations on the number of part-time coaches that I can have, which is a big key to our success.

Recruiting By the Numbers

With no athletic scholarships, my philosophy is that we have to "recruit numbers." For example, we don't have a "number one recruit" in a weight class, unless they are an extremely good student also and we have a chance to get them in on an academic scholarship. We don't have a number one, number two or number three recruit or so on. Although I've never coached at a Division I or Division II level, my guess is (at least in our sport), that they will have a number one recruit. If Joe doesn't take their scholarship, then they'll go to Frank, who is their number two recruit.

In contrast, we have to recruit a handful of wrestlers at every weight class with the hope of getting one. Our recruiting philosophy is to outwork the opposition. It's to recruit year-round and to be one of the first schools that a student looks at. I really do believe "the early bird catches the worm" philosophy.

The last part of our recruiting philosophy is that we feel we are going to be able to compete with other schools (even Division I and Division II schools) for blue-chip athletes. At the Division III level, there's sometimes the mentality that we "clean up after the big dogs eat." I don't believe that. In fact, we want to go head-to-head with the Division I schools for a blue-chip athlete for our top recruits. We lose several of these top recruits to those schools. However, when we do get them, we gain credibility, respect and exposure.

If you recruit an athlete like that and he doesn't choose you, we've also found that we have an opportunity to get him at a later time, if he decides to transfer. Probably one-quarter of our recruits every year are transfer students.

> **"We start with a recruiting base of 600 athletes. We call 300 of those personally."**

We generally have a recruiting base of 600 student-athletes. We contact 300 of those prospects personally, usually a phone call where we're speaking to the recruit directly. We don't count letters as a personal contact. We have 40 to 60 of those athletes visit our campus and we will get about 10 to 15 of them every year. I don't think I've ever had less than 10 recruits. The most recruits we've ever had in one year was 28. That was when we really sold the fact that we lost nine senior starters and there are only 10 starting positions in wrestling.

A Systematic Method to Identify Prospects

First of all, we identify our prospective student-athletes. After a lot of trial and error, we've developed a systematic approach to recruiting. It starts with an identification of our resources. I had to find out how much work-study money I had so I could have students help me with the phone calls, mailings and campus visits. Then I had to find out how much recruiting money that I had. It's money that I get from the admissions office.

I can generally go anywhere I want to recruit, as long as it's within driving distance. It also has to be directly associated with recruiting – for example, a competition or a home visit. All of my phone calls are paid for also, through the school code that I can use in my offices. In our athletic department, we share our offices. I'll bring in my coaching staff and/or student-athletes and we're able to get on eight phones at once. We just key in a code number and it gets charged to admissions, so we don't have to bill-back to our personal phones. We also have calling cards.

We rely on volunteers. I consider faculty or staff members to be volunteers. For probably 15 percent of our campus visits, we use a faculty or staff member if that student-athlete is interested in a certain major area. If not, we usually forego the faculty/staff visit with the prospective recruit. We are also in a position where we can use our alumni. Our alumni base is extremely strong. If I have a hard time getting an athlete to come to campus, I may have some of our alumni call them and talk to them about their major, if the student has a major in mind.

I worked really hard to get one of our prospective student-athletes to come to campus. For a while, he wouldn't come for a campus visit. We have a rule that we don't do home visits unless they come to campus first. We don't even do high school visits unless they come to our campus first. It's just kind of a rule that we've used. We found that a lot of students will say, "Yeah, it's okay to come to my high school and see me," or "It's okay to come to my home," but then we still have a difficult time getting them to campus. So we try to make sure that he's at least committed enough to come to our campus before we'll go to their home or to their high school.

We use alumni in an attempt to get them to come to our campus and we also use our alumni if they've already visited campus and they're on the edge. One prospect was very interested in accounting. He met with an accounting professor while he was on campus. Then he met with one of our most outstanding accounting alumni, who passed his CPA exam on the first try, all four sections of it. I think every little bit helps when you're dealing with blue-chip athletes.

> **"Every little bit helps when you are dealing with blue-chip athletes."**

Coaches as a Resource

I have six assistants. This is where it helps not to have any limitations on part-time coaches. I'm in an excellent position. I only have two paid assistants and one work-study assistant. I also have three assistants who are volunteers. About the only finances they receive from the college for their time is $15-20 every weekend and meal money to travel with us. They also get at least half of a bed free when we're on the road.

My assistants' responsibilities for the recruiting process are that they make a lot of phone contacts. We make a lot of phone calls. If I am recruiting a student, I call 100 percent of them. I might also write initial letters and do follow-up letters and things like that, but I also have to be on the phone with them. I talk with them on the phone before we set up the campus visit. I personally set up the campus visit with every single one of the athletes that come to our campus.

Student-Athlete Involvement

We use our student-athletes to help with some of the phone calls and all campus visits. We encourage prospects to bring people along with them. We set up the visit initially by talking to them on the phone. Then I'll write them a letter confirming the day and time they are coming and I'll add a P.S. on the bottom in bold that says, "We really encourage you to bring your parents along because we really feel that college decision is a family decision." I'll follow that up with a phone call before or after they get that letter, encouraging the parents to come. So generally, there's a commitment from the parents that they're going to come to visit a college with their son or daughter. Many times they have to take off work and plan ahead, so we make sure they know we want them to come. We like to recruit the whole family.

Recruiting Locally

I use a centralized recruiting base. Through trial and error, we've decided that unless it's a referral, we only recruit in the state of Minnesota. That's so I can stay a little more focused. We recruit all Minnesota participants in the state wrestling tournament. We will also follow up on all referrals from coaches – actually, any referral from an alumni, faculty or staff member, a student-athlete or parents. We kind of have a golden rule that we follow up on every single referral that we get.

> **Our golden rule is that we follow up on every referral that we get."**

I think it creates a good relationship with people, and we think it's really important because we have no athletic scholarships. We get right at it and follow up on those referrals as soon as we possibly can.

How am I going to recruit them? Number one, we send out a coach's letter. If I know about another athlete that I'm interested in from that school, I will tell the coach that I am interested in so-and-so and do you have any others? What I need to do is gather information as soon as I possibly can from the coaches. I think the coaches *like* to help out. I usually get about a 60 percent return from my first coach's letter. From my second coach's letter, I get about another 20 percent.

In the fall, my coaching staff calls every single wrestling coach in the state of Minnesota. We may just say, "Thanks for the referral" or "Here's what we are up to right now." We gather information. We use what we call a "recruiting card." We put every athlete on a handwritten recruiting card initially. We basically do everything manually until they visit campus and then we get computerized. We take those 600 initial cards and narrow them down to 300 really quickly, because many of the referrals we get can be screened out. Maybe they're not a good enough student or maybe we don't have a major that they're interested in. By the fall, we're only working with 300 cards, instead of 600.

The objective of our phone calls and our letter writing, at least initially, is to get information on the student-athlete. After that, we want them to visit campus. As I mentioned, we will not go to their home or their high school until they have visited our campus.

I personally sign every letter that I send out. I also address the letters. I put my last name under the Augsburg College return address so they know it came from me. It also shows that I'm the one addressing the letters. They also know I'm personally signing those letters. They also start to recognize my handwriting.

The coach's letter I send out goes out in June. We do a lot of follow-up student-athlete letters in July and August. Those are to follow up either the information that we have gathered on the student-athlete or information that the coaches have given us.

Our biggest effort is in September and October. Most prospects come for a fall visit. We don't ever pay for an athlete's visit. But fall campus visits have been very effective for us.

In September and October, we get together and make calls every single Wednesday night. I organize the list of phone calls with the full-time people in the athletic office on Monday and Tuesday. I actually plan which coach is going to call which other coach or which student-athlete. Then I do all the follow-up stuff that I need to do on Thursday and Friday and I start again the next Monday and Tuesday for the next Wednesday.

During the season, every one of our coaches gets four of our recruiting cards or four coaches to call. We make four phone calls per week. I use the number four because I can sell my assistants on the fact that it's one phone call per night, Monday, Tuesday, Wednesday, Thursday. Then they get another new four cards or four coaches to call the next week. We try to stay on that during the season. But that's really about all we're capable of doing.

The Minnesota Connection

My coaches are all from Minnesota, so I get them scheduled to call their area of the state. They call the coaches or athletes from their area of the state. I think that's a really important part of our recruiting; they are usually well-known in their area of the state. Unless he's a new coach to the sport of wrestling in Minnesota, I don't think there's one coach that does not know my staff or me personally or know at least a little bit about our program. That's why our recruiting base is only in Minnesota; that's where we have the most success.

We tried Wisconsin one year, which is our neighboring state, but we found that it really wasn't worth our while because our niche was really the state of Minnesota.

We send out letters whenever we can. We try our best to either make a phone call about every two weeks in the fall, or to get something in the athlete's hands about every two weeks about our school, about Augsburg College.

Through the Minnesota Wrestling Coaches Association, I have the home address and the school address of every single head wrestling coach in the state of Minnesota. So in June, I send a mailing to the coaches at their home addresses asking them for information on a specific individual or maybe just some referrals that they could give me about athletes either on their team or in their area. I think that really helps because most of the coaches have some time off in the summer and they have a little time to fill out that form. In the fall, I send another letter to them at the high school address if they haven't responded.

Crunch Time

We don't have many campus visits during the season, unless it's a competition visit, where we have athletes come in and watch us compete. Our real crunch time is basically in March and April, which is kind of nice because it's somewhat condensed. Out of 40-60 visits, we try to get 10-20 visits made in the fall. A lot of that is because of the time demands for student-athletes. The high school state wrestling tournament is the first week in March. We have a condensed period of two months before our school gets out in mid-May to get our recruiting done.

Gathering Information

Our number one objective is to try to get a prospect's phone number. We'll call a coach or the school or somebody who will give us a phone number. After that, we get an address and the parents names and all the rest of the information we can possibly get. But our biggest key is that we have to find out what kind of grades they have. We have to find out their ACT scores, their high school ranks and what their grade point average is.

> "Once we know their grades, we have more options."

Once we know their grades, we have more options. At our school we have a "Regent's Scholarship," so anybody who is ranked in the top 10 percent of their high school class is eligible for a base academic scholarship of $1,500. It goes to $4,500 if they're a valedictorian or in the top 1 percent of their class. They also have scholarships based on ACT scores, starting at an ACT score of 23 and going up to the highest score. They can get $1,500 to $4,500, depending on their score. When you walk into a campus visit and you congratulate a student on qualifying for your regent's scholarship at $4,500, it's a nice way to start the visit at a school that cannot offer athletic scholarships.

We really do a lot of research to gather this information. Our big information-gathering stage begins when our recruiting base goes down from those 300 cards to about 100 or less. There are a lot of non-qualifiers. We come from a strong academic school and there's just a lot of students who can't get in.

We know our admissions standards and so we must decide who to recruit and who to spend our time on. If you have a campus visit and go through that whole process and don't have a chance of getting the student accepted, it really is a waste of time.

There are a couple of other things that might be a determinant. We're a city school, so if somebody is looking at agriculture, we have to wish them luck and be on our way. We have to have a major that meets their needs. About 60 percent of our prospects are "outstate" students; they're not from the city. We don't do the high school visit or the home visit first, because we want to make sure that they're willing to come to the city in the first place. I don't need to travel five or six hours to outstate Minnesota to find out that a student really doesn't want to go to school in the city.

> **"Our academic standards require that we know who we can – and can't – recruit."**

We don't ask them that directly, because if you ask a student, "Are you interested in coming to school in the city?" sometimes they think there is a hidden meaning to that. We just have a roundabout way that we use in telephone conversations on selling the city. A lot of our graduates work in the city as a result of the internships they've had at our school. They have career opportunities there because of the access to the metropolitan area.

Factoring in Financial Aid

My coach's letter focuses on academics, but also we ask them to let us know about anybody that they think would qualify for a lot of financial aid. With room and board, tuition and fees, our school costs about $18,000 a year. So we talk about money freely, starting with our first phone conversation.

You had better be ready to talk finances when you make your phone calls, and we are. Our average financial aid package at Augsburg – including grants and scholarships, loans and work-study – is $13,500. Using those figures, which are researched by our financial aid department, we're able to at least keep parents or a recruit interested for a time when they might have discounted us just because of the cost initially. We use the figures that the college provides us.

We're looking for low-income, single-parent families many times, because generally those are students that get high financial aid awards. Academics are also important because the Regent's Scholarship and ACT-based scholarships use those criteria. We also have a Presidential Scholarship which offers free tuition and fees for four years as long as the student maintains a certain grade point average. We encourage our students to apply for any and all scholarships the college offers. The only downside of our presidential award is that if a student doesn't get it, they have their first negative feeling about Augsburg College.

The Campus Visit

Because everybody is really crunched for time in their work schedules, we set up campus visits by phone and then we send a reminder letter out. In bold letters within the body of the letter, we restate the date and time. We will also send a map. We also make a reminder phone call the night before, giving them verbal directions and talking to the family about the visit. A reminder call assures that we don't sit around waiting for a student to arrive when he or she forgot or has to reschedule.

Our campus visit is generally three hours. Our campus visits aren't business-like, but at the same time they are well-planned. We try to make the recruit feel like he's been our only visitor all spring long. The fact of the matter is, we have three recruits come each day. We have them come in at 9:00 a.m., noon and 3:00 p.m. We have a three-hour visit planned for each recruit. They will meet with an admissions counselor at the admissions office for about half an hour.

> **"If you miss more than two study groups, you can't wrestle."**

Then we talk about academics. Our athletes are required to participate in study groups three nights a week. Our study groups are led by our seniors, captains and upper classmen. If you do not attend study groups, you get two misses. If you miss more than two, you can't wrestle. That's our rule. So when wrestling practice starts on November 1st, you cannot wrestle if you have more than two misses. That means they can't come to practice and they can't compete.

We've found that the more discipline and structure that we have in our wrestling program, it carries over into how we treat the players off the mat. Initially, we usually get some grumbling and some complaints about the structure. But we've found that athletes like discipline, particularly when they see the results of it.

After I get done talking to them about the school year, then they go on tour with team members. Our admissions office has a rule that I can only pay one athlete for a tour. He gets one hour's pay for giving a family a tour. I don't believe in one-athlete tours. I believe we should have as many athletes as there are members of the family. So if mom, dad, a brother and the recruit come in, then we'll have four tour guides.

On Tour

I don't like dead time on a campus visit. I want everybody to have a chance to visit with each other while the tour guide is talking about the facilities and the academic programs. I've built into our lettering policy, you have to give so many campus tours in a year. There are exceptions. There are some athletes that I don't want giving campus tours to my prospective student-athletes. Maybe they are too quiet. For them, I have different requirements. They might come in and help me with mailings or something like that if they're not going to do campus tours.

We have a campus tour dress code. It's kind of common-sense stuff. We even allow them to wear hats as long as the hat is an Augsburg hat. We want to make sure that they are clean-shaven and that they're not chewing (tobacco). Even though they can't do that on an athletic site or in the gym, it's still something they do when I'm not around, so I make sure that I tell them that they are not allowed to do it on tours. I ask them to dress nice and be presentable. We have an exact tour map that we follow. We go to the same places with each campus visit. We give them a step-by-step tour information sheet. We actually have a meeting with all of our tour guides in regard to the order they will follow. I don't assume that it's going to be done right – I make sure it will be done right.

We also talk about things not to talk about. Basically I have two rules. No negatives and we don't talk about other recruits. I don't like recruits to see each other on campus. I don't like to talk to recruits about other recruits. In the sport of wrestling, we are often asked, "How many other guys are you recruiting at my weight?" Well, the fact of the matter is, I'm probably recruiting six or eight other recruits at your weight class, because I'm maybe going to get one or two. But if you tell a family that, they think that they're just another number. I don't know how to get away from that entirely. It's a situation where we have to tell them that "If you commit to us…as soon as you commit to us, the promise I can make to you is we won't contact any new wrestlers in or around your weight class." We can follow through with that.

> **"There are certain things we don't talk about on the campus visit."**

The Wall of Fame

For the rest of the tour they meet with me at the athletic facility. I take them to the wrestling room. We have a "Wall of Fame," which is photos of all of our All-American wrestlers. I take them through each one of the wrestlers and I introduce each one of the pictures to them, and tell them what that person is doing now in their life, what they're doing for a job and anything else. I think there's about 50 photos on our wall. We talk about practices, practice formats and schedules and I answer any kind of wrestling questions they might have. That's when I talk wrestling.

Then we go to eat, which is my favorite time. Not only because it's eating, but it's my favorite time to be with the families. It's very relaxed. It's a really social time. Then, when we're finished with that, I actually walk the recruit back to the admissions office or to their car. That's when I say good-bye. I really like that personal touch. I don't want my athletes to do that. I want to be the last person they see on campus.

We usually have plenty of time within that three-hour window. Admissions usually takes about half an hour, I take a half hour to talk to them, and the tour takes about 45-60 minutes. My wrestling room visit with the family generally takes about a half hour and then we finish it up with lunch. In March and April, I'm on to the next recruit. I have about half an hour between visits because admissions talks to them for that first half hour of the visit.

The Pitch

If a student decides that they're not going to go to Augsburg, we always make sure that we talk to them. We don't want to hear it from their mom or dad, even though that's fine initially. We always make sure that we have a phone call with that athlete so I can wish them luck personally. Then I send a letter. We call it the "no letter," but it also wishes them luck at the place that they're going to be going to school.

> **"We record the details of the visit, so we personalize our follow-up contacts."**

I always follow campus visits up with a very personal letter that says something about who they visited with. "I had a nice time with your mom and dad" or with your mom or with you and your girlfriend or whatever it might be. That's one of the things that we try to do to personalize the recruiting process.

We also record the details. On the initial recruiting card, we write down who the tour guides were and any details that came up. Because of our condensed recruiting time, things get hectic during those two months, so we make sure that we write down everything. We copy the cards. We use the front and back for notes that we take, so you can write very personal letters afterwards. It's really important for us to know where the student is in the whole process – if they've applied, if they have submitted their application essay and if they have sent their high school transcript. All these things have to happen in order. For us, even the financial aid materials have to arrive in a certain order for them to get their award.

Speaking of financial aid, we can't even talk financial aid with the family unless they present their financial aid award to us first. If I ask a family, "Have you received your financial aid award?" and they say yes, I ask, "Do you want to talk about it at all? Do you have any questions about it? Do you want to share it with me?" It's up to them whether they do or not. If they do, I can help explain it. That's particularly important for families that haven't had students go through the process before. It seems to be somewhat complicated until you explain it to them.

Early Contact

One of our keys to success is being one of the first schools that contacts a student. We like to be a sprinter initially, or one of the first ones to contact the student. But we've found that we need to stay persistent. We call it "sealing the deal." We become a marathon runner. I have to stay in it for the long run. If I do not make my phone call once a week to the prospects who are still interested in us, I have a good chance of losing them. They'll forget about us or they will think we're not interested and they may make a decision without considering us. We really try to stay in the race by sticking with things in the summer.

We don't "sign" recruits. The way that we have a good idea that we are going to have someone come to our campus is the deposit. However, even if they've committed to us, deposited to us, signed up for classes with us and went through the orientation session, until they are in class the first day of school, we have nothing to hold them to us except their loyalty and their word. That means that we still need to make follow-up phone calls about once every two weeks just to see how the family is doing, see how summer wrestling is going, how the summer job is going, whatever it might be, because we could actually lose that athlete up until the first day of school. It's never over until the first day of school.

Author Profile: Jeff Swenson

Jeff Swenson is head wrestling coach at Augsburg (MN) College. A four-time National Coach-of-the-Year award winner, his teams have won five NCAA Division III national championships. The 1979 Augsburg graduate has produced over 145 national champions, All-Americans and national Scholar-Athletes combined. He also serves as assistant athletic director and head strength coach for the athletic department.

Selling the Student-Athlete During the Campus Visit

by Jerry Wainwright

Because of changes in the NCAA rules, particularly with regard to home and campus visits, we have re-evaluated our total recruiting situation. The rules have really changed how we recruit players. I think the same effect could be detected nationwide. I think it's going to be very difficult to keep up with the "have's." The distance between the "have's" and the "have not's" is going to grow, not just in athletics, but in the economy, as we recognize what we have, compared to other people in this country. You are competing against programs that may have more resources – people and money – than you have. Other factors, in addition to rule changes, have changed recruiting.

I think the television exposure that certain teams in this country get dictates what happens in recruiting. Whatever your ideas may be about campus visits or home visits, television exposure really changes it. Of course, the condensing of the calendar does, too. It's very, very difficult to go out and do some of the things we used to do in the time we have available.

At Wake Forest, we had difficulty getting prospects to visit our campus – even prospects we ended up signing. Part of that was due to our school. We only had 2,900 students. Wake Forest is a private institution in the Atlantic Coast Conference. When I was there, our academic requirements sometimes worked against us. Not necessarily our admissions procedures, but what students had to take. Because of this, we had to be a little more aggressive in our recruiting.

First, Find Prospects to Recruit

When I first started coaching, an older coach told me, "There are only two good places to coach. One's at an orphanage, because there are no parents, and second, a prison, because there are no alumni." I've been trying to get a job at one of those two places for years. I haven't had any luck yet.

My first three jobs were in schools where there were already players. I got a very good head coaching job in high school at a very young age because of a death on the faculty and we won all kinds of games. Boy, I thought I was the greatest coach ever.

Then I took a job that offered more money, but there weren't any great players and we were 1-4 right away. Figuratively speaking, I was poised on top of the bridge, ready to jump into the river, when one of my older assistant coaches came by. He told me something that I've remembered for more than 20 years. He said, "Son, you can't have a circus without any animals."

I thought about that for a while and I realized he meant "Good coaches win with good players." Nobody wins with bad players. That old belief that a good coach can win with bad players isn't true. That doesn't happen anymore. If it does, it's a freak happening. It just sets you up to get fired, because it gives a false sense of hope to those 15,000 assistant coaches that are in the stands. It makes them think that there's a sense of reality that isn't true.

Involvement in the Recruiting Process

So recruiting, as we are talking about it – all the way from the phone calls through the close – is very, very important. To be a good recruiter, you have to be able to laugh and you have to be able to cry. At times, whether you are in the home or on campus, you also have to be able to *act*. I think one of the things that happens is we get so emotionally involved in recruiting that we don't do some of the things we *need* to do. We don't act.

> **"We get so involved, coaching becomes more than a job – it's a way of life."**

We are so subjective in how we look at what we do for a living. We take things personally and we get totally involved. The highs and lows of what we do are so critical to us. Coaching becomes more than a job – it's a way of life. Sometimes, people outside of coaching don't understand that. They say things like, "It must really be great. You guys have nothing to do in the spring but play golf."

One of the things I try to impress upon our alumni is that recruiting is a 12-month, 24-hours-a-day proposition. There is really no other way to look at it. But I think one of the things that we wind up doing as a result is that we spend too much time thinking about the prospect rather than covering what we know best.

Volume Recruiting

I heard Abe Lemons say one time, "The best way to solve the recruiting problems in college basketball is to give every coach in the country the same amount of money to recruit and tell them they can keep what's left over." I thought that was a heck of an idea. Except we all don't have the same amount of money. We don't have the same budgets. We don't necessarily have the same opportunities to do what a lot of people might call "volume recruiting." You have to have a team. You have to have bodies. You have to have the numbers. To do this, you compromise certain aspects of your recruiting to field a team.

Before I first got into college coaching, I coached high school for many, many years. I was very lucky. I coached seven high school All-Americans, so I knew a lot of so-called "big time" coaches. They said, "Jerry, why do you want to get into college coaching?" I said, "I don't know. The players are older. I think it might be a good thing to do."

They said, "Well, I don't know why you'd want to do it." We talked a little bit. I asked, "What's the worst thing about recruiting?" They said, "Campus visits." One guy turned to me and said, "It's 48 hours of hell." I said, "C'mon. What can be so bad for 48 hours?"

Now that I know better, I admit that it can be, absolutely, unquestionably, the worst 48 hours in your life. It can also be the best 48 hours of your life. The pressure in that 48 hours is incredible. The timing of where that campus visit comes in the recruiting process makes it worse. As a result, the cardinal rule that we live by is, "Never, ever have a prospect on campus officially unless you're willing to take him." Believe me, you end up turning down a lot of people.

But to me, if you do the right thing during the campus visit, you have an opportunity to get a commitment. As a high school coach, I always used to ask, "If this youngster right here wants to come, will you take him? Right now? I have him in my office. Right now, if he wants to come, will you take him?"

If there was any hesitation at that point, as a high school coach, I knew my player was not a primary recruit. So I don't do that to prospects. I never invite anybody we're not willing to take.

The second rule we follow is, "We will never, ever bring a prospect on campus unless we believe we're one of his top three choices." We don't want him on campus unless we're in his top three. You're better off waiting and saving visits and doing a good job with the ones you have, rather than being one of five choices.

> "The campus visit can be the worst 48 hours in your life. It can also be the best 48 hours."

We have one other thing that supplements our two cardinal rules. We never recruit anybody we can't get. I know that's a hell of a statement. I'm very lucky. At Wake Forest, we were in a big league. We had beaten the national champion. We got to play against some very good schools. As a representative of the Atlantic Coast Conference, we had the opportunity to get involved with a lot of prospects.

But the only prospects we want to be involved with – to the point of even thinking about home visits and campus visits – are prospects we have a realistic opportunity to get. Not to *recruit*, but to *get*.

The Campus Visit: Evaluating Prospects

There is such a wide variety of people involved with helping players choose a school now. I remember when I started in this, the parents would say, "Okay, coach, you do it or we'll do it."

Now there's the high school coach, the parents, and even Mr. Smith from the BBQ place down the street. I've been on home visits where you needed a rental hall to fit everyone in. I've been to smaller weddings than some of our home visits. The variety of input players get is unbelievable.

So the first thing I want to find out immediately is, "Who's going to make the decision?" It might be the mom. It might be the dad. You might guess wrong. It might be the girlfriend. It might be the boyfriend. It might be the high school coach. It might be any one of a number of people. If at all possible, I want that person on our campus in order to make our recruiting effective. I'm talking legally. I'm not flying in girlfriends or anything like that.

It's amazing, when you invite the right people, how willing they are to come. If they don't make an attempt to come, you probably guessed wrong on who's going to have input in this decision. I've always felt that's a good way to feel out who's really going to have input in the process.

Don't Make it a One-Time Thing

Second, repeat exposure to your campus is a good idea. The best way to make an official visit go well is to have an unofficial visit prior to that. The more times prospects can get on your campus unofficially, the better chance you have of signing them.

Wake Forest is in North Carolina. It was tough to get a kid from California to visit us unofficially. We had five of the best California players come through our campus. Of course, they also swung up I-40 and visited Duke and Carolina, but at least they stopped by.

With an unofficial visit, we have a much better feel for that youngster and he has a much better feel for us. There are definite advantages to unofficial visits. One, there's no time limit. There's no 48 hours. You have time to hang out. It's personal time. There's no agenda. The player gets a chance to see who you really are. It's not forced. Much more importantly, you get to know what they really are like. The more someone comes, the more I feel that we have a chance of getting the player. We want them to come and see our players. We want them to come and do things on their own. Bring your mom, bring your brother, whatever. Bring them to meet the coaches.

> "When you are recruiting, don't restrict yourself to only the best players in the state."

We try to get prospects on our campus when they're young. You can do it through your games. You might have procedures where you invite the best players in the state to your games. Don't restrict yourself necessarily to the best players. If you work through teams or through coaches, be patient. Someone from the team or a coach might be coming and then all of a sudden, the third or fourth time, they bring your prospect along.

You can get prospects to your campus by hosting your own camp. The women's teams in North Carolina did a great job on this. They had all these specialty camps. Post player camps, guard camps, little mini-camps. You get a lot of prospects to come. Particularly if they are low-cost camps. Players want to come. They want to learn about specifics to their position. It can get prospects on campus. I know there's a difference between having a camp and recruiting a prospect on your campus. But I've always felt "the more he or she sees, the better."

Also, anytime you get a prospect on your campus unofficially, try and get him into the admissions department. Our admissions people like to do an interview as well.

One year, we signed three recruits who had only been on unofficial visits. They never had an official campus visit. The school was comfortable with all three because they had been through admissions. They knew who they were; it wasn't just a transcript anymore. They had discussions with them. They had a little meeting with them. They went through the catalog with them. They talked to them. All of which is legal. If you're lucky enough to get a prospect there unofficially, don't just show them the weight room. Take them over to admissions. At some point, that may save you an official visit.

The Pre-Visit

There's one thing I think has really helped us. I call it a "pre-visit" with the prospect. I don't want any surprises when recruiting a prospect, so I try and gather as much information about the prospect as possible. One high school coach asked me, "Are you really a coach or do you work for the FBI in North Carolina?" I told him, "Well, as a coach, I don't want to wake up in the middle of the night with my head coach knocking on my door saying, 'Somebody did something. How come you didn't know about it beforehand?'" With the decreased number of evaluations and the limitations on phone calls, a lot of what we're doing right now has to be

based on information collected from third-party sources.

I want to know everything. When I go to visit a school, I always go down to the lunchroom and ask the women down there, "Does this kid ever say thank you?" It's unbelievable the insight I've gotten into prospects from people like that. Honest insight. High school coaches sometimes inflate how good the prospect is, "Yeah, he's a really great kid." Don't rely on them totally; they can be biased.

As you find out more about prospects, it really helps you with the visit. I ask prospects all kinds of questions. If the prospect doesn't respond, you've still learned something. There's an old saying that I really believe, "You can modify behavior, but you can't rehabilitate character." Don't get the idea you will be able to change someone *too much*.

> **"You can't change the spots on a leopard. You can't change them too much."**

We can *modify* behavior. If I get a player who is used to getting up at 7:00 in the morning, I can modify his behavior. If I want his toes on the line or I want him to hit the elbow on every cut, I can modify his behavior. I cannot rehabilitate character. I can't put my ego in the way and say, "I'll change the spots on the leopard." I want my players to talk. That's a hard business. If you have a prospect who's sullen or doesn't talk or doesn't communicate, how are you going to teach him to talk on defense? How is he going to talk and communicate with professors?

The Pre-Visit Process

So I ask prospects a million questions. What do you like to do? Who's your favorite basketball player? I have a whole list of questions I go through. Every time I talk to him, I interrogate him. I do the same with the coach and the parents. Of course, I ask them each different questions. Parents love to talk, especially about their children. I also talk to their friends. Anybody I can talk to, I do.

Then I build what I call a "visit profile." It includes interests, things he likes, doesn't like, food preferences, whatever. Then, prior to his visit, I come back to him and I tell him exactly what to expect. I tell him, "We have these events going on. You'll need this amount of money to go to those events. Would you like to go see Aerosmith? You're going to need $20 to buy a ticket. We can't buy it for you. If you want to go, you need $20 for that ticket. If you want to buy something from the bookstore, here is the cost."

I even fax the bookstore price sheet to the high school coach. I don't want the prospect coming here uninformed. I want him to know right up front.

I think most people appreciate that. They know what clothes to bring. Maybe there's some event where he needs a sport coat and a dress shirt. I've had prospects arrive with a little gym bag. Other players come with trunks. Usually, it's based upon the neurosis of their parents.

I also tell the prospect exactly what's going to happen. I tell them, "These are the guys on the team you'll be staying with. This is where you'll be staying. This is where you'll be eating. These are the events on campus this weekend." I tell him. I don't just send the itinerary. I prep them. I call that the pre-visit process.

Getting the Prospect to Campus

Transportation is another issue. There are many decisions you have to make in regard to transportation. Especially when you are flying prospects in, don't make the major part of the first day travel. The 48 hours doesn't start until they get there, so don't wear them out trying to get them to your campus in a hurry. It amazes me, in retrospect, how dumb I've been in the past about this issue.

I used to try to get them out of school Friday early and then they would travel all day. Then they would stay out late Friday night and be absolutely worn out the rest of the weekend. They're tired; they're irritable. All they're thinking about is sleep, especially if it's the second weekend visit in a row. They are much better off taking the first available flight out on that Friday after school (or that Thursday after school, if they're coming in to see classes), whatever the preference may be. Put them up off campus. Don't let them come to your campus until the next day, when they are fresh.

One of our best visits was a prospect who came from Idaho. I met him in Chicago. We had to stay in Chicago a day and then we traveled together the next day. I really got to know him. That kind of travel time for a coach, I think, is a great opportunity. Being in a car is not that bad. If you're within four hours, it's not a bad situation to be in.

Use Your Players Wisely

We all know our best recruiters are our players. If you've got good kids, you'll get good kids. You just have to get the prospects to campus. If you've got good players, I don't care if you're 2-25 and in a rebuilding situation. It doesn't matter. Kids sell kids. You have got to get your young prospects involved in the campus visit right away. They're going to be with those people, they're going to compete against them for playing time, they'll live with them and, hopefully, they're going to win with them.

> **"Get the prospect involved right away."**

Gather Team Intelligence

We have a meeting at the beginning of every year with our new recruits. We ask, "What did you like at other schools on your visits?" Remember, these are our players now. They chose us, so we ask, "What are the things you liked best at other schools? What did you like best at our school? What was the best part of your visit and what was the worst part of your visit?"

I also do the same things with their parents and with their coaches. I keep a running file. We talk about it every year. Even if a player is a senior, he goes through the whole thing again with us. He might have gone to camps, he might have been with development teams, or talked to other players.

We tell them to talk to other players and then we ask, "What did he say about his visit? What do you remember?" We try to build a file of "the good, the bad and the ugly."

We practice our visits. If we are having a prospect in on Friday, we will have a meeting early in that week. We hand out a profile on that player to the team. It contains all the information that we have collected. We talk about the prospect who is coming in. We outline the do's and the don'ts. We make everyone on our team part of it. Not just our stars, not just our captains, but all of our players.

At the end of the discussion, I pick up all the papers and I give them a test. Nickname. Girlfriend's name. City, state, high school. I want our freshman guard, who never plays, to go up to that prospect, who has a great opportunity to take his position for three years, and say, "Hey, John, you had a great season last year up there in Buffalo, didn't you?" If he can't do that for us, we cannot win. He should not be in our program. The first responsibility of our play-

> **"The first responsibility of our players is to help us get good players."**

ers is that they continue to help us get good players. That may sound cruel, but every one of them talks about playing on an NCAA team. The only way you play on an NCAA team is to keep corralling those players. So make it part of their job. Our players are accountable for getting other players. We don't just verbalize it. We practice it.

Get Non-Athletes Involved in Recruiting

The next segment of practice is with the student body, not just our players. With computers, I am able to find people from the same hometown, the same area. I find people that have the same interests. I find people that might have the same leisure interests, the same religious interests. I meet with student body leaders on campus – sororities, fraternities and student government. I tell them point blank, "We need you." We're a very small campus. That's both good and bad. I tell them, "You need to be part of John Smith's visit. John Smith is not just going to be with basketball players. He's going to be with you. We want you to spend 10 minutes with him." I say, "Jimmy Jones, you're from Buffalo; Bobby Fitzgibbons is coming in from Buffalo. I want you to stop by the office. I want you to talk to him about how you get back and forth. Are you ever going to be able to share a ride?"

It's unbelievable how much the students on campus have helped us. One of the biggest things that we're all trying to do in today's times, is meld. Well, we've gotten a lot of good public relations out of this. We've done a pretty good job of recruiting with our student body.

Then we go to the campus people: the professors, other coaches, and administrators. I give them the opportunity to be involved. I've met with small groups; I've met with departments. I say, "Here's what we're trying to do during the campus visit. Do you have any ideas? What can you do to help?" They can be a great source. People look at things differently than we do. Sometimes it helps you focus. They want to be a part of it.

Sometimes we don't use all the people we can use. Sometimes we should use them more often. They have a great perspective. Tennis coaches. Golf coaches. Football coaches. They can all help you. There might be a payback required later on, but you know, you're all on the same page.

Prepare Third-Party Recruiters

In all those situations prior to the visit, when we are working with third-party recruiters, I will meet with them individually. Then we have what we call a "team meeting" – a campus visit team meeting.

> **"Get your campus community involved. It will give you rapport with people."**

In other words, let's say the prospect is coming in on Friday. That Wednesday or Thursday, we'll call a meeting. There might be 10 or 11 people who are going to be involved with it, within our campus community. Legitimate recruiters, not boosters. They will all be there and we will talk about the youngster. Who does what, who's going to attack what. Who's going to talk about what. We try to build kind of an "esprit de corps." If nothing else, it gives you great rapport with some of the people on the faculty and it's been very, very positive for us.

Use other athletes, both male and female. Players – even prospects – influence other players. I remember the year we went 4 for 4, we signed one of the players in North Carolina who was lesser known, but he came to every official visit. He wound up starting at center for us his senior year. He did a great job. He was a developmental player. But what a guy. When he was a high school senior, he was telling other high school seniors, "Hey, I really want you to come to play here. We can get it done. We can turn this program around."

Housing Arrangements

Some campuses have very bad dorm situations. If you put prospects up in a hotel, technically, it's supposed to approximate campus living. Try to find a hotel that approximates campus living in most towns and you surely wouldn't send anybody there, much less somebody you're trying to sign.

There's a very famous coach in our league who had many of the prospects stay at his home. I don't know if that's the best way to do that. I really don't. I think that's one of the things you need to hash out before the prospect arrives. Maybe he spends a day in the hotel and a day in the dorm. If necessary, you move a player out of the room or they double up. That's how they wind up anyway.

I think you have to look at the mechanics of a campus visit. I think you should have every minute accounted for. You have to balance activities. Here's our academic advisor. Okay, now we're going to meet with the English teacher. Now we're going to go here. Before you know it, the kid is anesthetized. He doesn't work that hard in high school. That's too many meetings. I think you have to vary activities so that doesn't happen. Do something serious, then balance it right away with something a little bit lighter, maybe something with the players. Let's go watch a player work out in the weight room. Or go over to the dorm and talk to some residents.

> **"You can be tempted to want to get all the 'bad stuff' out of the way."**

I know a lot of times, you're tempted to get all the bad stuff out of the way first. But then your prospect has such a sour taste about it, it's hard to come back to the good stuff. I like to punch and counter punch. But I have a supplementary plan. We must have Plan A and Plan B. Every minute must be accounted for. When I say *every minute*, I mean I write down every minute. I have student assistants pace out how long it takes to get from here to there so I can have a gauge.

If you tell somebody you're going to be there at 1:00, and it takes 10 minutes to walk there, and the guy's done at five 'til, he's going to be late and now we're going to be rushed. I think you have to be right on the money in these things. Plan ahead.

But don't be too rigid. Sometimes things go really well and you don't want to interrupt them. You have to have backup plans. We make that a part of that meeting that we have with all the people who are going to be involved with the prospect. We sketch out a Plan A and a Plan B. We build in a contingency in case they're having a good time. If that's the case, I'm not going to interrupt them. But let's plan a backup time we can get together if that happens.

Don't make things up on the fly. That's when you stumble around and things just don't go very smoothly. Be prepared. I think the biggest thing you want is for anybody who's going to have contact with the prospect to *know* him. It's amazing how a prospect's eyes light up when someone knows who he is.

The Sell

The most important part of the campus visit is a segment that tells prospects what we are going to do for them. What are we going to do for you? We show prospects instructional tapes that we have made ourselves with our own players.

After we do the instructional tape, we have splices of what happens in a game. Here's a player working on a crossover move, which he didn't have when he came in here. These are the drills we use with this player, both on his own and under coaching situations. We film them in the pre-season practice. We film them in individual workouts. We tape them. Then we splice them out. Here he is, crossing over against another team. He went from *here* in practice to *there* in the game.

Don't just talk about player development; *show* a player's development. This has really worked for us. At the end of each year, we document it. We work with the campus communications department. They have people in radio and TV who come over and have a mock interview with our players.

"Tell us about your high school background," we ask.

"I'm from Far Rockaway, New York. My junior year I scored 43 points a game. My senior year, I was at Oak Hill Academy; we were number one in the country."

Then we ask, "What happened your first year here?"

He says, "I played 22 minutes the whole season. I wasn't strong enough. Coming from high school basketball, it was very hard on me." The player verbalizes his freshman year, from where he started to where he ended.

We use those tapes on our campus visits. The host player can show his tape. Now, all of a sudden, the prospect starts to think, "These players got through it. They're not afraid to talk about their weaknesses and strengths." It's amazing how we develop conversations out of that. It's really helped our players.

Show them what you have to offer. Prospects are interested in your equipment, certainly the shoes that you wear. The academic support you have. Your schedule. Not just this year, but who you're planning on playing in the future.

Now, the second part of this is what the player will do for you. We say, "Son, if you decide to come here, here's what you're going to do for us." We show them class options and talk about what we expect out of them academically. For example, we have a rule that if you miss a class, the whole team runs at 5:00 in the morning. We tell them that. The other players tell them that. We tell them what we're doing for them, and what they will do for us.

> **"Show them what you have to offer."**

The Close

For me, the campus visit is all about closing. It's like selling the clearcoat finish on the car. You are at the point where you want that prospect to feel so good about what you're all about that it gives him the confidence to say, "I'm coming." Campus visits, to me, are visual and emotional. What the arena looks like. What the fine arts building looks like. Who my teammates will be. The close must be both visual and emotional to be effective.

Remember, recruiting doesn't end when the prospect leaves campus. The best thing you can do after the youngster leaves is to follow up. You have to follow it up. If it was good, you keep it good. Pound the positive. Quiz them. Get feedback and then pound that. Make it affirmative. Make it easy for them to choose you.

Author Profile: Jerry Wainwright

Jerry Wainwright is head men's basketball coach at the University of North Carolina-Wilmington. Highly regarded as a program builder, the Coach-of-the-Year award winner has 15 years of college recruiting experience. His other coaching stops include Xavier University and Wake Forest University.

THE MENTAL EDGE BOOKSTORE

Competitive Excellence: The Psychology
and Strategy of Successful Team Building (Second Edition)

Retail: $23.95
Your Price: $21.95

A national best seller! A collection of top coaches from across the United States. Each coach is highlighted in sections on motivation, team cohesion, discipline, mental preparation, mental toughness, and communication. A valuable addition to every coach's library!

Basketball Resource Guide
(Second Edition)

Retail: $25.00
Your Price: $22.00

The most comprehensive resource medium for the sport of basketball. Includes listings for audiovisual tapes, books, magazines, research studies and more…The consummate book for the basketball junkie! *NOTE: Third edition is now available on computer disk only. Please inquire for further details.*

The Mental Edge: Basketball's
Peak Performance Workbook (Second Edition)

Retail: $29.95
Your Price: $26.95

The best mental training book for basketball on the market today! A step-by-step manual, teaching mental preparation and training for coaches and athletes. Chapters include goal setting, visualization, stress management, concentration and more…

Psychology of Winning
Notebook

Retail: $25.00
Your Price: $20.00

The complete notes from Steve Brennan's highly-acclaimed Psychology of Winning Clinic. Topics include motivation, discipline and mental toughness. So organized, it's just like being at the clinic!

Golf Psychology
Workbook

Retail: $25.00
Your Price: $22.00

The core text of Steve Brennan's Golf Psychology Workshop for the Competitive Golfer. An in-depth exploration of the mental side of golf for someone who takes the game seriously. It could help you drop a few strokes from your game!

Mental Edge Clinic
Workbook

Retail: $30.00
Your Price: $25.00

The core text of Steve Brennan's nationally-acclaimed Winner's Edge Clinic for coaches and athletes. A tabbed, 3-ring binder containing the most recent research in the field of performance enhancement. Includes an Appendix section, including an extensive list of bibliographical data.

(Please reproduce this order form for additional copies)

THE MENTAL EDGE BOOKSTORE
Preferred Customer Order Form

BOOKS	QTY.	UNIT PRICE	TOTAL
Competitive Excellence	_____	$21.95	_____
Basketball Resource Guide	_____	$22.00	_____
The Mental Edge	_____	$26.95	_____
Psychology of Winning Notebook	_____	$20.00	_____
Golf Psychology Workbook	_____	$22.00	_____
Mental Edge Clinic Workbook	_____	$25.00	_____
Postage/Handling (Continental US only)		$5.95	_____
(Canada and Foreign Only)		$15.95	_____
Total Amount Due:			_____

Name: _____

Address: _____

City: _____ State: _____ Zip: _____

Home Phone: _____

METHOD OF PAYMENT:
☐ Check enclosed, made payable to **Peak Performance Publishing**
☐ Visa ☐ Mastercard

Card #: _____

Expiration Date: _____

Signature: _____

☐ Please Send Me a FREE Recruiter's Library™ Catalog!

> *All monies in U.S. Currency Only.*
>
> Make check payable to: *Peak Performance Publishing*
>
> and mail to:
> **Peak Performance Publishing**
> **14728 Shirley Street**
> **Omaha, NE 68144 USA**

For Credit Card Orders, Call Toll Free (800) 293-1676

MEET THE *Inside Recruiting*™ STAFF

Steve Brennan

Bridget Ann Weide

Jon Brooks

STEVE BRENNAN is the editor and publisher of *Inside Recruiting*™: *The Master Guide to Successful College Athletic Recruiting.* As President of Peak Performance Consultants, an international education and motivation company based in Omaha, Nebraska, he specializes in motivation, mental preparation and education, and performance enhancement strategies catering to student-athletes, coaches, educators and business people.

Steve has written other coaching-related books which are listed in the Mental Edge Bookstore form on page 140. He is included in the *World Sport Psychology Sourcebook, World Sport Psychology Who's Who, Who's Who in American Education, Two Thousand Notable American Men, Who's Who in the World,* and the *International Who's Who of Business Entrepreneurs.*

Currently, Steve is the executive director of The Recruiters Institute™, the director of The Recruiters Library™, and the founder and executive director of the Midwest Youth Coaches Association. Steve has been a performance consultant with the Kansas City Royals baseball organization and has experience as a basketball analyst on the Creighton University Radio Network.

Steve's clientele includes professional and amateur athletes and coaches, corporate leaders, professional organizations, and all persons striving for peak performance in their lives.

BRIDGET ANN WEIDE provided the layout for *Inside Recruiting*™: **The Master Guide to Successful College Athletic Recruiting.** As co-owner of Image Building Communications in Omaha, Nebraska, Bridget provides writing, editing, layout and design services for a variety of small businesses and organizations in the greater Omaha area. She received her degree in Public Relations from the University of Nebraska at Omaha in 1996. In addition to this book, Bridget produced *The Life and Times of Jesus of Nazareth* by Judd Patton as well as numerous newsletters, journals, and other publications.

JON BROOKS was responsible for editing, cover design, and layout design assistance for *Inside Recruiting*™: **The Master Guide to Successful College Athletic Recruiting.** An avid sports fan, Jon also co-owns Image Building Communications in Omaha, Nebraska. He graduated with honors in 1996 with his degree in Public Relations from the University of Nebraska at Omaha. Jon provides layout and design for numerous newsletters, publications and organizations. He is an editor of *Nebraska Life* magazine.